GREEN FINANCE STRATEGIES FOR POST-COVID-19 ECONOMIC RECOVERY IN SOUTHEAST ASIA

GREENING RECOVERIES FOR PEOPLE AND PLANET

OCTOBER 2020

Notes:
In this publication, "$" refers to United States dollars.
ADB recognizes "South Korea" as the Republic of Korea and "Vietnam" as Viet Nam

Cover design by Edith Creus.

Left side from top to bottom: Essential food packs provided to the most vulnerable households under Bayan Bayanihan program (photo by Eric Sales/ADB); President Masa Asakawa visiting ADB-supported slum upgrading and green infrastructure projects in Makassar City, South Sulawesi, Indonesia on 2 March 2020 (Photo by Ariel Javellana/ADB); Philippine Army soldiers distribute food packs to residents of Barangay Hulong Duhat in Malabon City, Metro Manila (photo by Veejay Villafranca/ADB);

Center photos from top to bottom: Fishermen exploring the waters for a catch in Malekula, Vanuatu (photo by Eric Sales/ADB); Plants along the shores of East Tanjung Plnang, capital of Riau Islands Province, Indonesia (Eric Sales/ADB); Biodiversity Corridor project for the preservation of the Bidoup Nui Ba National Park (photo by Lester Ledesma/ADB).

Right side from top to bottom: Burgos Wind Farm seen in the background in Ilocos Norte, Philippines (photo by Al Benavente/ADB); BTS Skytrain at the heart of Bangkok's commercial and business neighborhood (photo by Lester Ledesma/ADB); Solar panels and turbines at the Burgos Wind and Solar Farm in Burgos, Ilocos Norte in the Philippines (photo by Al Benavente/ADB).

Contents

Contents

Figures and Boxes

Foreword

Governments across Asia have deployed a significant amount of emergency capital in response to the coronavirus disease (COVID-19) pandemic, with an initial focus on protecting lives and livelihoods. The next stage of the crisis will require governments to prepare long-term recovery and stimulus packages to support economic growth and employment security.

These plans will need to carefully factor in existing vulnerabilities in developing member countries, now further exacerbated by COVID-19 impacts. Countries in developing Asia were already facing the triple threats of climate change, biodiversity loss, and declining ocean health before the pandemic. In many major Asian cities, air pollution and water scarcity are already highly visible. Coastal populations, especially along Southeast Asia's long coastlines, are increasingly vulnerable to sea level rise and increasingly frequent typhoons. The linkage between health impacts, natural disasters, pandemics such as COVID-19, and changes in the climate, oceans, and forests is becoming more evident. An example is greater human incursion into animal habitats, creating a higher risk of animal viruses infecting humans.

Within this context, recovery strategies must not reverse past gains made in protecting a country's natural environment and inadvertently end up supporting a growth in fossil fuel or carbon-intensive investments leading away from the Paris Agreement's target trajectory. Conversely, there is a critical window of opportunity to reset how we orient our economy and build back better. The member states of the Association of Southeast Asian Nations (ASEAN), for example, have already set a target of generating 23% of their primary energy from renewable sources by 2025, as opposed to a 9.4% share in 2014 (and currently estimated at meeting around 15% of demand). The need for large capital flows of finance to achieve such targets whether in renewable energy, nature-based solutions, or other infrastructure sectors, is more critical now, as these can be engines of sustainable growth providing socioeconomic benefits. Strategies that catalyze green finance from both public and private sectors to resilient projects that create sustainable jobs, should be the centerpiece of post-COVID-19 economic recovery pack ages.

The Asian Development Bank (ADB) has been working closely with governments across Asia and the Pacific in deploying an assistance package of $20 billion to help countries counter the severe impact of the COVID-19 pandemic and address the urgent needs of the sick, the poor, and the vulnerable. For Southeast Asian countries, ADB has provided direct COVID-19 related assistance of $5.4 billion. In parallel, ADB is also supporting projects such as the Geodipa Geothermal Project in Indonesia that will help spur recovery.

This document helps to further identify examples of policies and green finance mechanisms that can both crowd in much-needed capital from across the world, as well as bring a critical focus on the sustainable use of our natural resources. I hope some of these mechanisms will provide practical support toward the development of green and sustainable recovery plans for the region.

Ahmed M. Saeed
Vice President for East Asia, Southeast Asia and the Pacific
Asian Development Bank

Key Messages from Peer Reviewers

Koen Doens, Director General, International Cooperation and Development (DEVCO), European Commission. The coronavirus disease (COVID-19) pandemic has shaken the world to its core, testing health-care and welfare systems, our societies and economies, and our way of living and working together. The European Union (EU), together with its Member States and European Development Finance Institutions, as Team Europe, have so far mobilized recovery packages of nearly €36 billion with the objective of tackling and mitigating the health and socioeconomic consequences of the COVID-19 pandemic. Team Europe promotes a recovery that puts us all on a sustainable path, allowing us to address the risk of growing inequalities and climate change, while embracing the opportunities offered by digital technologies. We need international partnerships to build a green, digital, resilient, and socially just recovery. To realize these objectives, the EU has called for a global recovery initiative to build back better. Only if we work together will we have a chance to harness those drivers of change and turn them into opportunities to emerge in better shape. Sharing the same values and objectives, the EU and the Asian Development Bank (ADB) can not only assist the countries of the region in facing the current health and economic challenges, but also contribute to enacting the recovery in a way that is more environmentally friendly through, among others, the promotion of sustainable finance. One excellent example is our recent cooperation with the ASEAN Catalytic Green Finance Facility, a project designed by ADB in support of Association of Southeast Asian Nations (ASEAN) members' climate change and environmental sustainability goals with an EU contribution of €50 million.

Jorge Moreira da Silva, Director, Development Co-operation Directorate, Organisation for Economic Co-operation and Development (OECD). For the global COVID-19 recovery to safeguard against future pandemics, drive sustainable growth, jobs, and investment, it has to be green. Green finance, green systems, green policies. Now is the chance to do better for people and the planet. I commend ADB for its timely work to help pave the way for a more resilient and sustainable future in the region.

Seth Tan, Executive Director, Infrastructure Asia. This work by ADB is very timely. In a disrupted world, there is opportunity for countries to re-double efforts to traject toward their green and sustainable development goals, while at the same time, contribute to economic recovery. As a regional infrastructure facilitation office under the Government of Singapore, InfraAsia is pleased to work with ADB to help raise the awareness of the solutions available to catalyze further green and sustainable infrastructure. Private sector investment and financing remains available and very keen to deploy into quality green infrastructure even in current times. The sharing of good examples of "how to" catalyze more green and sustainable infrastructure within this report could be very useful to inspire governments to create more enabling environments to attract more international private sector into their country's projects.

Sean Kidney, Cofounder and Chief Executive Officer, Climate Bonds Initiative. The COVID-19 pandemic is having a crushing impact on the lives of millions of our people. We are going to have to work hard on recovery. It will be challenging. Job creation must be paramount. But in recovery we have to bear in mind what our scientists are telling us: climate change is going to bring us many more shocks, including more pandemics. We have to recover with resilience in mind, and green transition center stage: achieving our climate goals will reduce the risk of catastrophic shocks in the future. We need to build back better. That means green infrastructure to improve productivity, building projects where we drastically cut energy needs, land restoration jobs to strengthen the natural environment, and investing in resilient health systems. The recovery will need capital. Lots of it. A huge opportunity exists with green finance to tap the trillions of dollars from global institutional investors looking for green and sustainable investments. Working closely with the ADB, the Climate Bonds Initiative stands ready to support ASEAN governments in rebuilding economies, helping citizens, and creating a sustainable and resilient future for us all.

Nick Robins, Professor in Practice, Sustainable Finance, Grantham Research Institute on Climate Change and the Environment, former Co-director of UN Environment Inquiry into a Sustainable Finance System (2014–2018). It is imperative that we build a green and inclusive recovery out of the COVID-19 crisis, not least in Asia where the urgency of a shift to sustainable development is particularly pressing. What is striking is the demand from businesses, investors, governments, and citizens for practical solutions that are fast, job-rich and aligned with future-facing sectors of the future. This is the first global crisis where green and sustainable finance can make a real difference. Here, multilateral development banks, such as ADB, have a pivotal role to play at times of crisis to provide both confidence and competence. This paper expertly sets out the rich menu of options that governments, businesses, and investors now have before them to make the recovery green and inclusive. I hope that these options are deployed at speed and scale in the months ahead.

Preety Bhandari, Chief of Climate Change and Disaster Risk Management Thematic Group concurrently Director, Sustainable Development and Climate Change Department, Asian Development Bank. The COVID-19 pandemic and ensuing shock on economies across the world has brought into stark focus the already critical issues of poverty, inequality, the environment, and the changing climate and how inextricably these are linked. It is evident that the design of recovery interventions will be crucial, as decisions made now will create systems, institutions, and assets, and define development directions that will last well into the future. It is thus vital that economic stimulus measures are cognizant of long-term, sustainable, and inclusive solutions that put us on a sustainable recovery pathway. The year 2020 was an important milestone for ratchetting up climate ambition under the Paris Agreement, and any deceleration and reversal of efforts made under the Paris Agreement commitments will likely tip the balance into decades of economic, livelihood, human, and environmental losses. Under its Strategy 2030, ADB has already led in setting targets for climate-related investments with a commitment to make 75% of all ADB projects climate-relevant and invest a cumulative amount of $80 billion from its own resources by 2030. This paper aims to accelerate those efforts by providing examples and concepts for green finance mechanisms that can be used to scale up the volume of not just public, but also commercial and private, finance that can and should be directed to green infrastructure-based recovery programs. I hope countries in the region pick up on some of these concepts for their green recoveries; ADB stands ready to help with knowledge and funds to take these further and deeper.

About the Authors

This document was prepared by an Asian Development Bank (ADB) team led by Anouj Mehta, unit head, Green and Innovative Finance and the ASEAN Catalytic Green Finance Facility (ACGF). The team included ACGF consultants Sean Crowley, Karthik Iyer, and Marina Lopez Andrich, working within the Innovative Finance Hub in ADB's Southeast Asia Department. The document was prepared under the overall supervision of Ramesh Subramaniam, director general, Southeast Asia Department, and has benefited from significant peer reviewer inputs and feedback.

Acknowledgments

The lead team of authors for this paper acknowledges the contributions made from members of the Asian Development Bank (ADB) Southeast Asia Innovation Hub and Association of Southeast Asian Nations Catalytic Green Finance Facility (ACGF) teams including, Joven Balbosa (advisor), Alfredo Perdiguero (director), Raquel Tabanao (associate knowledge management officer), Camille Bautista-Laguda (consultant, ACGF) and Naeeda Crishna-Morgado (consultant, ACGF). The team is grateful for the inputs from Amitabh Mehta (Indus Blue Consultants consultants, United Kingdom).

The team also thanks ADB specialists including Deborah Robertson (environment specialist), Kate Hughes (senior climate change specialist) and other specialists including Jane Zhang (principal communications specialist) and Duncan Mcleod (communications specialist).

Overall supervision was provided by Ramesh Subramaniam, director general, ADB Southeast Asia Department.

The team greatly benefited from the guidance and inputs provided by the following peer reviewers during conceptualization as well as the final draft stage of the publication.

Peer Reviewers and Advisors

- Jorge Moreira da Silva, Director, Development Co-operation Directorate, Organisation for Economic Co-operation and Development (OECD)

- Jens Sedmund, Head, Environment and Climate Change, Development Co-operation Directorate, Organisation for Economic Co-operation and Development (OECD)

- Seth Tan, Executive Director, Infrastructure Asia

- Sean Kidney, Cofounder and Chief Executive Officer, Climate Bonds Initiative

- Nick Robins, Professor in Practice, Sustainable Finance, Grantham Research Institute on Climate Change and the Environment, former Co-director of the United Nations Environment Inquiry into a Sustainable Finance System (2014–2018)

- Preety Bhandari, Chief of Climate Change and Disaster Risk Management Thematic Group concurrently Director, Sustainable Development and Climate Change Department, ADB

- Bruno Carrasco, Chief of Governance Thematic Group, Sustainable Development and Climate Change Department, ADB

- Bruce Dunn, Director, Safeguards Division concurrently Officer-in-Charge. Environment Thematic Group, Sustainable Development and Climate Change Department, ADB

- Tariq H. Niazi, Director, Public Management, Financial Sector and Trade Division, Central and West Asia Department, ADB

- Priyanka Sood, Senior Financial Sector Specialist, Central and West Asia Department, ADB

Abbreviations

ABS	–	asset backed security
ACGF	–	ASEAN Catalytic Green Finance Facility
ADB	–	Asian Development Bank
AFME	–	Association for Financial Markets in Europe
AIF	–	ASEAN Infrastructure Fund
ASEAN	–	Association of Southeast Asian Nations
ASCN	–	ASEAN Smart Cities Network
ASSURE	–	ASEAN Scaling Up Renewables + Storage
ASUS	–	ASEAN Sustainable Urbanization Strategy
CARES	–	COVID-19 Active Response and Expenditure Support
CBI	–	Climate Bonds Initiative
CDO	–	collateralized debt obligation
CFF	–	Climate Finance Facility
COVID-19	–	coronavirus disease
CPRO	–	COVID-19 pandemic response option
CRTB	–	COVID-19 Recovery Transition Bonds
DBS	–	Development Bank of Singapore
DBSA	–	Development Bank of Southern Africa
DNS	–	debt for nature swaps
EDC	–	Electricité Du Cambodge
EIB	–	European Investment Bank
ESG	–	environmental, social and governance
EU	–	European Union
FAO	–	Food and Agriculture Organization of the United Nations
MPA	–	marine protected area
GCF	–	Green Climate Fund
GDP	–	gross domestic product
GHG	–	greenhouse gas
ICMA	–	International Capital Market Association
IDFC	–	International Development Finance Club
IFI	–	international finance institution

IFC	–	International Finance Corporation
ILO	–	International Labour Organization
IMF	–	International Monetary Fund
IREDA	–	Indian Renewable Energy Development Agency
JTF	–	Just Transition Fund
JTM	–	Just Transition Mechanism
MDB	–	multilateral development bank
MW	–	megawatt
NDC	–	nationally determined contribution
PIC	–	private, institutional, and commercial
PPA	–	power purchase agreement
PPP	–	public–private partnership
PT SMI	–	PT Sarana Multi Infrastruktur (Persero)
PV	–	photovoltaic
R&D	–	research and development
SDG	–	Sustainable Development Goal
SGDF	–	Shandong Green Development Fund
SIO-GFF	–	SDG Indonesia One - Green Finance Facility
SOE	–	state-owned enterprise
TFCA	–	Tropical Forest Conversion Act
US	–	United States
USAID	–	United States Agency for International Development
WRI	–	World Resources Institute

1 THE COVID-19 IMPACT: CONTEXT AND SYNOPSIS

Plants along the shores of
East Tanjung PInang, capital of
Riau Islands Province, Indonesia.
(Eric Sales/ADB)

The coronavirus disease (COVID-19) pandemic has had a global impact on lives, livelihoods, and economies. With over 25 million confirmed cases and over 840,000 deaths worldwide (per the World Health Organization, 1 September 2020), the impact of the pandemic in terms of job losses and economic recession at national and global levels is expected to be significant. The Asian Development Bank (ADB) estimates that the global economy could suffer between $5.8 trillion and $8.8 trillion in losses, equivalent to 6.4% to 9.7% of global gross domestic product (GDP).[1]

Box 1: IMF Warning on Economic Fallout

The International Monetary Fund (IMF) has warned that the world should expect to brace for the worst economic fallout since the Great Depression of the 1930s. IMF Managing Director Kristalina Georgieva described the current crisis as "a crisis like no other," which "has disrupted our social and economic order at lightning speed and on a scale that we have not seen in living memory."

Source: IMF. 2020. Confronting the Crisis: Priorities for the Global Economy. 9 April.

Southeast Asia impact. Within the Southeast Asia region alone, ADB estimates that the impact of COVID-19 will generate losses to the region's GDP of $163 billion or 4.6% of the region's GDP for a short containment scenario and $253 billion or 7.2% of the region's GDP for a long containment scenario, and job losses from 11.6 million to over 18.4 million (footnote 1). ADB's *Asian Development Outlook 2020* estimates that the region's GDP growth in 2020 will now sharply decrease from 4.4% in 2019 to -2.7% in 2020, due to broad declines in consumption, investment, and trade.[2]

For example, in Viet Nam, an estimated 35,000 businesses have shut down in the first quarter of 2020 according to a survey conducted by the Vietnam Chamber of Commerce and Industry.[3] In the Philippines, an estimated 3.4 million formal workers have been affected due to COVID-19 related shutdowns.[4]

Relief efforts. In response, governments across the region are diverting budgetary funds for relief efforts, including cash transfer schemes, food supplies, expansion of social assistance programs, and acquisition of medical resources for COVID-19 prevention and control, with an estimated $315 billion (based on collating individual country information from the International Monetary Fund [IMF]) being spent on COVID-19 relief packages in member states of the Association of Southeast Asian Nations (ASEAN) region in the first half of 2020. Multilateral development agencies such as ADB have also been a major part of these government efforts with loan and grant funds deployed urgently, including through ADB's COVID-19 Active Response and Expenditure Support or CARES Program, funded through the COVID-19 pandemic response option (CPRO).

The European Union (EU), as part of its extended effort beyond borders, and its global solidarity initiative "Team Europe," is extending relief support to the most vulnerable and conflict affected populations across Africa, Asia, and the Pacific with an overall funding of over €20 billion.[5] Globally, it is estimated that over $11 trillion has already been set aside toward relief efforts.[6]

---

[1]   ADB. 2020. An Updated Assessment of the Economic Impact of COVID-19. *ADB Brief* No. 133. Manila. May.

[2]   ADB. 2020. Asian Development Outlook 2020 Supplement: Lockdown, Loosening, and Asia's Growth Prospects. Manila. June.

[3]   P. Van. 2020. Covid-19 Could Bankrupt 50% of Vietnamese Enterprises: VCCI. *VNExpress International*. 9 April.

[4]   M. U. Caraballo. 2020. SBWS Payout Hits ₱44B. *The Manila Times*. 15 June.

[5]   J. Borrell. 2020. "Team Europe"—Global EU Response to Covid-19 Supporting Partner Countries and Fragile Populations. *European External Action Service*. 11 April.

[6]   World Economic Forum and SYSTEMIQ. 2020. The Future of Nature and Business Policy Companion. 14 July.

From relief to recovery, the challenges. Almost 9 months into the pandemic, countries recognize the need to create longer-term economic recovery packages to address the challenges the pandemic caused. In compiling such packages, several conflicting pressures on government budgets have to be carefully balanced (Figure 1).

Figure 1: Balancing Relief, Recovery, and Rejuvenation

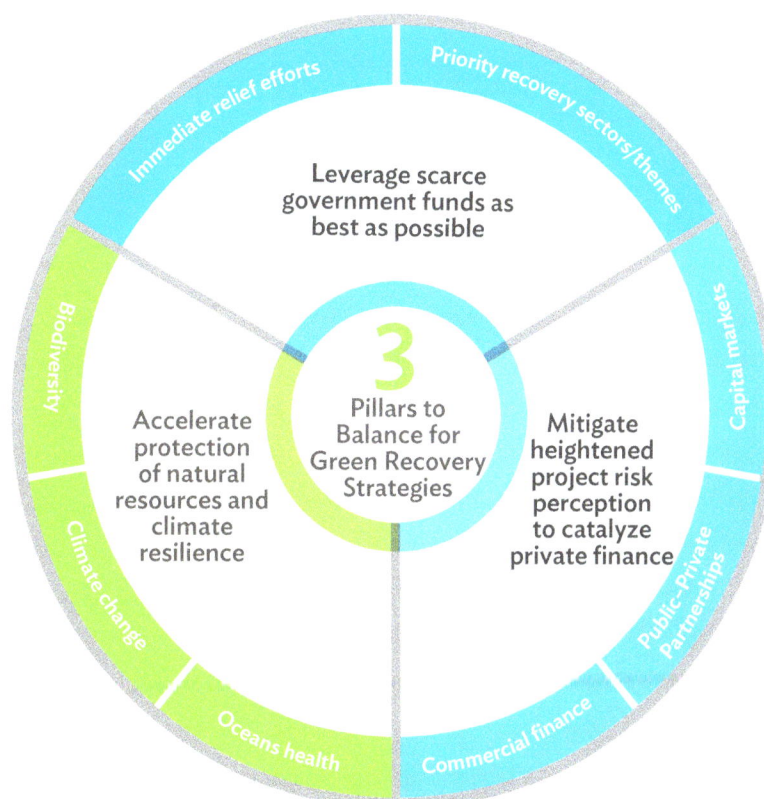

Source: Asian Development Bank.

Several countries in Southeast Asia were already in the high debt–to–GDP ratio bracket before the pandemic. This, in conjunction with reduced economic activity, increased capital outflows, and (possibly) increased borrowing costs, could threaten the ability to borrow further in the future. Some governments have also had to delay planned funding of critical infrastructure to cater to immediate relief spending needs.

The emerging need to assess investment reallocation and debt alleviation strategies could be an opportunity to revisit nature-based and sustainable solutions for more resilient physical infrastructure to mitigate climate change and physical risks. Several countries, such as Indonesia and the Philippines, have created task forces to explore strategic options for economic recovery and rejuvenation of economies.

Synopsis. Given this context, this paper aims to explore the rationale for a green recovery being at the heart of post-COVID-19 economic planning. A number of countries have already embarked on creating green recovery strategies, while green programs that had been in place pre-COVID-19 also provide a base to build upon, in other countries. Several of these examples are cited here including capital market mechanisms such as various types of bonds and de-risking funds created by various countries and ADB. Lessons learned from these examples and ongoing work in the post-COVID-19 era by the ADB team, including managing the ASEAN Catalytic Green Finance Facility (ACGF), perhaps the only regional green vehicle of its type in the world, have been built on to provide possible green finance concepts and mechanisms that could be used by countries to frame their own green recovery strategies and efforts.

2 A GREEN RECOVERY: CRITICALITY AND CHALLENGES

Burgos Wind Farm
in Ilocos Norte, Philippines.
(photo by Al Benavente/ADB)

5

Placing a "green recovery" at the core of all economic recovery strategies is increasingly seen as the best and only way for countries to rejuvenate their economies. Green in this context encompasses a number of elements, including sustainability of natural resources and climate resilience, as well as inclusiveness for all sections of society. Green infrastructure for a green recovery is an especially critical area to focus on given the scale of impacts that infrastructure development can and have had, both positive and negative.

Prior to the COVID-19 pandemic, the Global Commission on the Economy and Climate had concluded that strong climate action has the potential to generate over 65 million new low-carbon jobs by 2030, deliver at least $26 trillion in net global economic benefits, and avoid 700,000 premature deaths from air pollution.[7] The Global Commission on Adaptation estimated that investing $1.8 trillion globally from 2020 to 2030 in resilience building measures could generate $7.1 trillion in total new benefits.[8]

Box 2: Insights from Oxford Smith School of Enterprise and the Environment

Green construction projects can deliver higher multipliers. Clean energy infrastructure is helpfully very labor intensive in the early stages. One model suggests that every $1 million in spending generates 7.49 full-time jobs in renewable infrastructure, 7.72 in energy efficiency, but only 2.65 in fossil fuels. In the long run, these public investments offer high returns by driving down costs of the clean energy transition. Harnessing more of these opportunities could result in kick-starting the green innovation machine and driving an efficient, innovative, and productive economy, with higher spillovers that benefit the wider economy.

Source: C. Hepburn et al. 2020. Will COVID-19 fiscal recovery packages accelerate or retard progress on climate change? Oxford Smith School of Enterprise and the Environment. Working Paper 20-02. 4 May.

Post-COVID-19, studies from Joseph Stiglitz and Nicholas Stern have shown that a green recovery can maximize the impact of any stimulus (Box 2), asserting that "the COVID-19 crisis could mark a turning point in progress on climate change."[9]

A vulnerable world pre-pandemic. Even prior to COVID-19, several of these elements were already threatening equitable growth across the world including in the member states of ASEAN. This region has long been considered one of the most vulnerable on the planet, with increasing frequency of typhoons; rising sea levels; a long, exposed coastline; and urban water shortages often linked directly to climate change. The COVID-19 impact has only served to make a highly vulnerable population even more exposed.

Green recovery strategies would therefore ensure an acceleration of efforts to meet already existing threats and challenges, as highlighted further in the criticalities noted here, and not just spur immediate economic growth that might actually harm people, the environment, and the planet in the longer-term. As pointed out by the Coalition of Finance Ministers for Climate Action, a group of 52 finance ministers engaged in efforts to address climate change through economic and financial policies according to the six Helsinki Principles, "There can be no going back to the old normal."[10] It goes on to stress the need for rapid and targeted investment strategies that can lead to growth in jobs and a better future. These investments will need to be labor intensive in the short run, but with high multipliers and co-benefits.[11]

---

[7] The Global Commission on the Economy and Climate. 2018. *Unlocking the Inclusive Growth Story of the 21st Century: Accelerating Climate Action in Urgent Times. Key Findings and Executive Summary*.

[8] Global Commission on Adaptation. 2019. Global Leaders Call for Urgent Action on Climate Adaptation; Commission Finds Adaptation Can Deliver $7.1 Trillion in Benefits. 10 September.

[9] C. Hepburn et al. 2020. Will COVID-19 Fiscal Recovery Packages Accelerate or Retard Progress on Climate Change? *Oxford Smith School of Enterprise and the Environment Working Paper* 20-02. 4 May. p.4.

[10] The Coalition of Finance Ministers for Climate Action. Helsinki Principles.

[11] The Coalition of Finance Ministers for Climate Action. 2020. *Better Recovery, Better World: Resetting Climate Action in the Aftermath of the COVID-19 Pandemic*. July.

A. The Four Criticalities

The four key aspects underlining the need for a green recovery strategy, especially as pertaining to infrastructure development, are shown in Figure 2 and outlined further in this section. While catalyzing capital can be seen as an input into the other three "outputs," it still needs to be addressed in framing a green recovery strategy, so the four criticalities are inextricably linked.

Figure 2: A Fourfold Rationale for Green Recovery

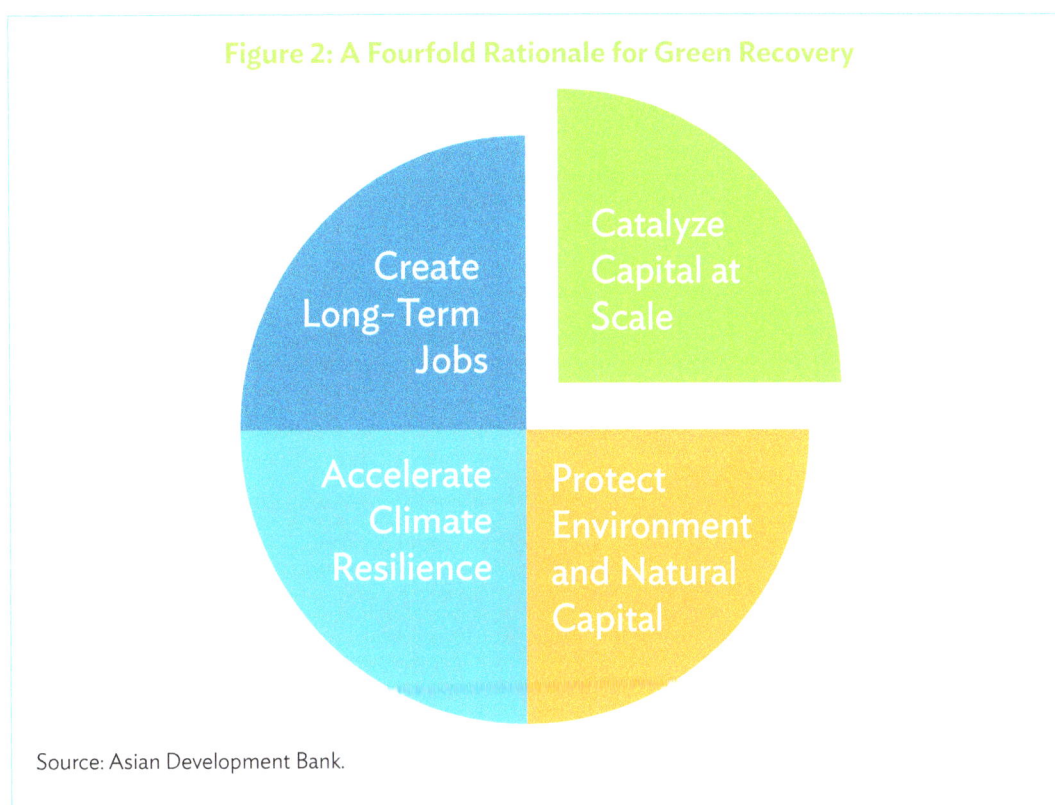

Create Long-Term Jobs

Catalyze Capital at Scale

Accelerate Climate Resilience

Protect Environment and Natural Capital

Source: Asian Development Bank.

1. Job Creation Criticality

One of the outcomes of the pandemic has been the impact on the weakest and poorest, particularly women and young people; this demographic has been the worst hit with high job losses, especially in the informal sector. The International Labour Organization (ILO) reports that 1.3 billion people work informally in Asia and the Pacific—65% of the world's informal employment, with around 7 in 10 workers in developing Asia working in the informal economy. Informal employment accounts for the highest share of total employment in South Asia (89%), followed by Southeast Asia (76%) and Central Asia (70%). Within the informal sector, women make up a larger share in low- and lower-middle-income countries, at 92.1% and 84.5% respectively (versus 87.5% and 83.4% for men). [12]Additionally, the ADB and ILO estimate that young people's jobs in Asia and the Pacific will be hit harder than adults' by COVID-19, with youth unemployment rates projected to rise in 2020, doubling in some countries. Some 10 million to 15 million youth jobs (full-time equivalent) may be lost across countries in Asia and the Pacific in 2020.[13]

---

[12] ADB. 2020. COVID-19, Technology, and Polarizing Jobs. *ADB Briefs* No. 147. August.
[13] ADB and ILO. 2020. *Tackling the COVID-19 Youth Employment Crisis in Asia and the Pacific.*

Sustainable and secure job creation thus has to be a key goal of recovery strategies whether created directly (e.g., infrastructure construction projects) or unleashed indirectly as ancillary economic activities (e.g., trade in agribusiness commodities or ancillary tourism activities).

Economic regeneration has become especially important to support a large number of displaced daily wage workers, impacted small and medium-sized enterprises, and rural areas often with reverse migration of workers. To this end, investment in reskilling, building new skills, and income protection will take center stage as will the requirement for revised labor laws and standards that are equitable.

Recent thinking on post-COVID-19 recovery has highlighted the positive impact of green stimulus packages in creating jobs and keeping businesses afloat, and has included "clean physical infrastructure investment" among key policy recommendations for the achievement of economic and climate goals.[14]

The Organisation for Economic Co-operation and Development has noted that green policies can not only support job creation in numerous green economic sectors through a transition of the economy toward more labor-intensive services sectors, but also mitigate the impacts of job destruction that occurs when dirty or polluting industries are closed or replaced by green industries or products, as is gradually happening in several countries. Similarly, a widely-cited model estimates that every $1 million in spending can generate 7.49 full-time equivalent jobs in renewable energy infrastructure and 7.72 jobs in energy efficiency, compared to 2.65 jobs in fossil fuels.[15]

> *A low-carbon recovery could not only initiate the significant emissions reductions needed to halt climate change, but also create more jobs and economic growth than a high-carbon recovery would.*
>
> **World Economic Forum**

The importance of green recovery strategies is highlighted by the World Economic Forum, which identifies 15 systemic transitions with annual business opportunities worth $10 trillion that could create 395 million jobs by 2030 while also paving the way toward people first and environmental development that will be resilient to future shocks.[16]

A recent McKinsey report provides an analysis of the impact of stimulus on a European country. It suggests that mobilizing €75 billion to €150 billion in capital for an economic stimulus package focused on a low-carbon recovery could yield €180 billion to €350 billion of gross value added. Such a package could generate up to 3 million new jobs, while also enabling carbon emission reductions of 15% to 30% by 2030.[17]

2. Natural Capital Criticality

Unencumbered industrialization and the push for growth at the expense of natural resources and natural ecosystems have been the cause of visible and rapid degradation of natural capital in preceding decades. This has been evident in both urban and rural areas, on land as well as at sea.

Depleting oceans and forests. Destruction of natural resources not only threatens lives but is also inextricably linked with climate change. Deforestation and illegal and over-mining have also created the severe risk of future

---

[14] *Smith School of Enterprise and the Environment.* 2020. Building Back Better: A Net-Zero Emissions Recovery.

[15] H. Garrett-Peltier. 2017. Green versus brown: Comparing the employment impacts of energy efficiency, renewable energy, and fossil fuels using an input-output model. Economic Modelling, Elsevier. 61(C). pp. 439–447.

[16] World Economic Forum and AlphaBeta. 2020. *The Future of Nature and Business.*

[17] H. Engel et al. 2020. How a Post-Pandemic Stimulus Can Both Create Jobs and Help the Climate. *McKinsey & Company.* 27 May.

disasters, including rising convergence of human and wildlife contacts, resulting in the potential transmission of further deadly viruses. The world's oceans have been acting as giant carbon sinks, absorbing about a third of the carbon dioxide emissions generated by human activities since the beginning of the industrial revolution. However, the oceans are also now faced with a massive rise—by as much as 30% according to some estimates—in seawater acidity since the industrial revolution.[18] The estimate that the current rate of ocean acidification is 10 times faster than at any point over the preceding 55 million years is highly sobering.[19]

Southeast Asia's cities and rivers are perhaps the most visible manifestation of the impact of overusing and polluting natural capital resources. Over half of the plastic entering the world's oceans can be traced back to five growing economies, four of which—Indonesia, the Philippines, Thailand, and Viet Nam—are in Southeast Asia.[20] Plastic pollution in the oceans impacting marine biodiversity has already been highlighted with ramifications for not just the health of coastal communities but also on fishing-related local economies. With an estimated over 3 billion people dependent on seafood as a source of animal protein, and a global fishing market approaching $150 billion by 2023, the impact and the need for action is critical.[21]

Restoring this balance using interventions both at or near the seas, such as Marine Protected Areas (MPAs), wastewater management, sustainable coastal ecotourism, or land-based interventions, such as climate smart agriculture, urban greening, and constructing conservation spaces and green corridors on land, are some potential solutions. More transitional changes in hitherto "brown" sectors would include greening manufacturing and packaging, where a commitment to renewables and a circular economy can provide green dividends and long-term resilience by alleviating the impact on natural capital. MPAs have demonstrated a remarkable impact on organism size (e.g., by 28%) and fertility leading to higher egg output and quality leading to replenished fishery stocks.[22] Studies on snapper fisheries in New Zealand demonstrated benefits of 14 times more fish in fully protected MPAs than in fished areas, with egg production at an estimated 18 times higher than outside the protected area.[23]

These and other nature-based interventions can hugely support natural resource protection, regeneration, and long-term resilience with key sectors prioritized for recovery strategies depending on local circumstances.

3. Climate Change Criticality

Perhaps the largest universal themes impacting every country, including those in Southeast Asia, are managing climate change and enabling climate resilience. These are also perhaps the most critical elements for any green recovery strategy to address.

The Paris Agreement. Almost every country signed up to the Paris Agreement (within the United Nations Framework Convention on Climate Change) in December 2015 to jointly commit to best efforts (targets set for both climate mitigation and adaptation) to keep the global temperature rise in this century well below 2 degrees Celsius above preindustrial levels and to pursue efforts to limit the temperature increase even further to 1.5 degrees Celsius. The 1.5-degree target is the threshold per the Intergovernmental Panel on Climate Change, beyond which we are likely to see lasting and permanent changes to our climate, including more frequent and intense impacts such as heatwaves and storms.

---

[18] Government of the United States, Department of Commerce, National Oceanic and Atmospheric Administration. 2020. Ocean Acidification.

[19] K. Simpkins. 2020. Ocean Acidification Prediction Now Possible Years in Advance. *Science Daily.*

[20] McKinsey & Company and Ocean Conservancy. 2017. *Stemming the Tide: Land-Based Strategies for a Plastic-Free Ocean.*

[21] Global Fishing Watch; and M. Shahbandeh. 2018. Global Seafood Market Value 2016–2023. Statista. 27 March.

[22] M. Cooney, M. Goldstein, and E. Shapiro. 2019. How Marine Protected Areas Help Fisheries and Ocean Ecosystems. *Centre for American Progress.* 3 June.

[23] T. J. Willis, R. B. Millar, and R. C. Babcock. 2003. Protection of Exploited Fishes in Temperate Regions: High Density and Biomass of Snapper *Pagrus auratus* (Sparidae) in Northern New Zealand Marine Reserves. *Journal of Applied Ecology.* 40. pp. 214–227. 8 April.

> *Dramatic strengthening of the nationally determined contributions (NDC) is needed in 2020. Countries must increase their NDC ambitions threefold to achieve the well below 2°C goal and more than fivefold to achieve the 1.5°C goal.*
>
> **United Nations Environment Programme**

The reality. Despite this, economic growth has been at the cost of greenhouse gas (GHG) emissions. The 2019 United Nations Environment Programme Annual Emissions Gap Report highlighted the possibility of missing Paris Agreement targets, noting that even if countries were to meet their commitments, the world is headed for a 3.2-degree Celsius global temperature rise over preindustrial levels. This will likely lead to even wider ranging and more destructive climate impacts.[24] Intensive development as well as the loss of several carbon sinks—the water bodies and forests—negated the commitments made. Emissions of coal-fired power plants in Southeast Asia are set to triple by 2030 based on a Harvard-backed study.[25] ADB estimates that emissions in several ASEAN member states have increased at the same pace as economic growth over the last decade, driven by the high energy intensity of growth.[26] Despite commitments to renewable energy, the most rapid relative increases in the energy mix have come from coal and other carbon-intensive fuels. The escalating climate crisis has serious implications for broader environmental issues, with increasing waste, air, and water pollution across cities in the region.

Visible impacts. Over a third of the global annual 7 million premature air pollution-related deaths are in Asia and the Pacific.[27] This is stark evidence of the importance of climate change, compared even with the COVID-19 pandemic. Climate change and unsustainable development are also estimated to have caused $3 trillion in direct economic losses from disasters and 1.3 million deaths from climate-related and geophysical disasters from 1998 to 2017.[28]

ASEAN region at risk. The region has almost 600 million people living along long coastlines of around 174,000 kilometers, economies heavily dependent on natural resources, and a heavy reliance on agriculture and fisheries for livelihoods. It is considered particularly vulnerable to climate change impacts such as sea level rise, droughts, floods, and tropical cyclones, which are already increasing in frequency. Myanmar, the Philippines, Thailand, and Viet Nam rank in the top 10 countries most affected by extreme weather due to climate change in the last 20 years, according to the Global Climate Risk Index.[29] An ADB report in 2009 already projected that annual mean temperatures in Southeast Asia could rise by 4.8 degrees Celsius by 2100, leading to mean sea level rises of 70 centimeters.[30] This would result in the relocation of cities and people, which is already in evidence, and declining rice yields by 50%. A 2016 ADB report (footnote 26) noted that the economic cost of inaction, a loss of 6.7% of combined GDP by 2100, is already likely to be worse, with a projected 11% of GDP loss.

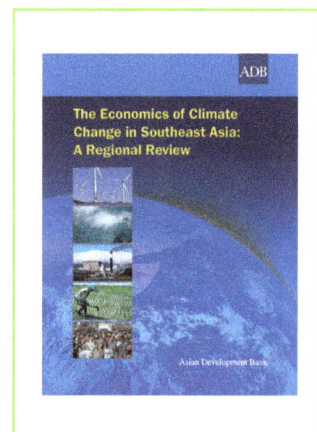

[24] United Nations Environment Programme. 2019. *Emissions Gap Report 2019*.

[25] S. N. Koplitz et al. 2017. Burden of Disease from Rising Coal-Fired Power Plant Emissions in Southeast Asia. *American Chemical Society*. 51 (3). pp. 1467–1476.

[26] ADB. 2016. *Southeast Asia and the Economics of Global Climate Stabilization*. Manila. January.

[27] World Health Organization. 2018. One-third of Global Air Pollution Deaths in Asia Pacific. 2 May.

[28] United Nations Office for Disaster Risk Reduction, Centre for Research on the Epidemiology of Disasters. 2018. Economic Losses, Poverty and Disasters: 1998–2017.

[29] D. Eckstein et al. 2020. Global Climate Risk Index 2020: Who Suffers Most from Extreme Weather Events? *Germanwatch Briefing Paper*.

[30] ADB. 2009. *The Economics of Climate Change in Southeast Asia*. Manila.

Climate change and health impacts. A United Nations report has highlighted how climate change is expected to exacerbate health problems that are already a major burden on vulnerable populations, including: (i) higher susceptibility to climate-sensitive health impacts for certain groups; (ii) high sensitivity of many infectious diseases, including waterborne ones, to climate conditions; (iii) climate change impacts on the length of transmission season and the geographical range of many diseases; and (iv) incidence of new and emerging health issues, including heatwaves and other extreme events due to climate change.[31] Malnutrition and undernutrition were highlighted as a concern for several developing countries. This link to possible future epidemics and pandemics adds further urgency to include climate change as a core recovery strategy.

The climate impact on the Sustainable Development Goals. Climate change is a critical theme cutting across almost all the Sustainable Development Goals (SDGs) and hence more impactful than if simply treated as one of the SDGs. As noted at the United Nations High-Level Political Forum on Sustainable Development in 2019, climate change can be a "threat multiplier with the potential to worsen some of humanity's greatest challenges, including health, poverty and hunger."[32] Addressing climate change through green recovery is thus integral to addressing the sustainable development challenges of each country.

4. Catalytic Capital Criticality

Even narrowing green recovery strategies to green infrastructure would still point to the overriding challenge of an adequate flow of capital to meet the needs arising from the previous three criticalities. This has been as true of the ASEAN region as in other developing economies. However, better prepared projects could be the catalyst to attract increased flows of global green capital.

In the bigger picture, the 2030 Agenda and the Paris Agreement are really about the same things. They provide our biggest opportunity for positive, systemic change that will ensure a resilient, productive and healthy environment for present and future generations.

Patricia Espinosa, Executive Secretary of the Secretariat of the United Nations Framework Convention on Climate Change, and Liu Zhenmin, Under-Secretary-General for Economic and Social Affairs of the Secretariat of the United Nations

Green infrastructure financing needs. Southeast Asia alone requires an estimated $3.1 trillion or $210 billion annually from 2016 to 2030 for climate change-adjusted infrastructure investments. However, with a financing gap estimated at $102 billion per year for selected Southeast Asian countries from 2016 to 2020, the need for private sector financing to fill the gap was already critical even before the pandemic.[33]

The COVID-19 impact on the financing gap. The COVID-19 pandemic has altered the financing landscape, with earlier estimates of government funds available for green infrastructure sharply reduced as government budgets are diverted to large emergency relief programs. For instance, in Indonesia, the government is exploring the reallocation of $3.9 billion from the 2020 budget for COVID-19 related measures.[34] Further, with increased risk perception from sharply lower revenue projections for most infrastructure projects, private capital flows—already in search of the few bankable projects in the sector—are also likely to be much more constrained, widening the financing gap. Figure 3 outlines the key conflicting challenges faced by most economies.

[31] United Nations Framework Convention on Climate Change (UNFCCC). 2017. Human Health and Adaptation: Understanding Climate Impacts on Health and Opportunities for Action. Synthesis Report by the Secretariat. Subsidiary Body for Scientific and Technological Advice 46th Session. Bonn. 8–18 May.
[32] UNFCC. 2019. *Impacts of Climate Change on Sustainable Development.* 19 July.
[33] ADB. 2017. *Meeting Asia's Infrastructure Needs.* Manila. February.
[34] A. W. Akhlas. 2020. $3.9 billion State Spending Reallocated for COVID-19 Response: Sri Mulyani. *Jakarta Post.*

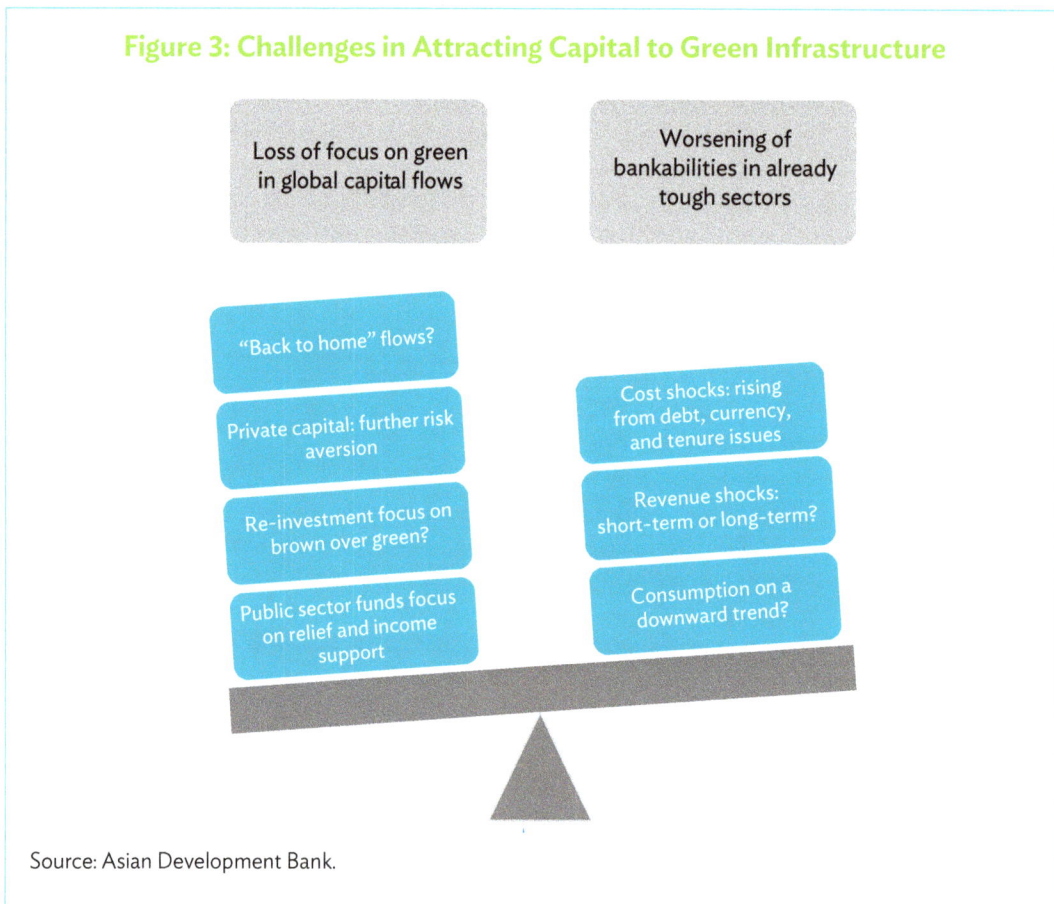

Figure 3: Challenges in Attracting Capital to Green Infrastructure

Loss of focus on green in global capital flows

Worsening of bankabilities in already tough sectors

"Back to home" flows?

Private capital: further risk aversion

Re-investment focus on brown over green?

Public sector funds focus on relief and income support

Cost shocks: rising from debt, currency, and tenure issues

Revenue shocks: short-term or long-term?

Consumption on a downward trend?

Source: Asian Development Bank.

It has been noted that the suddenness of the COVID-19 pandemic has had a severe impact on the global economy, with sectors such as airports seeing demand dry up. In a period of 2 months, daily commercial flights fell from more than 110,000 to less than 30,000. In April, national highway traffic levels in Java, Indonesia, plunged by almost 70%. But uniformly, across all sectors, the costs of service delivery are going up as governments rush to make service delivery pandemic-proof.[35] With such a scenario, there is a possibility of public–private partnership (PPP) contracts looking to terminate or renegotiate terms and conditions that could further widen the negative impacts on economies.

Emerging and developing economies, especially given the fiscal challenges as described above, coupled with capital outflows, run the risk of having onerous debt repayment obligations in the long term, and spiraling debt–to–GDP ratios, ratings downgrades, and the long-term dearth of capital sources due to the increased sovereign risk.

Attracting private, institutional, and commercial funds. To avoid such unsustainable scenarios, government recovery strategies must plan to better leverage their resources for attracting capital from various non-public sources including PPPs, institutions (pension funds, commercial banks, etc.) and the capital markets, together grouped as private, institutional, and commercial (PIC) sources. Mechanisms for leveraging or blending PIC funds should be especially developed to apportion risks that are best suited to each entity, whether government or PIC sources. Without such a clear understanding of the various risks and roles, needed capital flows will not occur, especially given the heightened risk perceptions by PIC sources post-COVID-19 in developing economies.

---

[35] S. Grover, H. Rahemtulla, and C. Gin. "Managing Public–Private Partnerships for a Post Pandemic Recovery." ADB Blog. 29 May 2020.

Multilateral development banks (MDBs) and international financial institutions (IFIs) can provide support to national and local governments in developing such mechanisms and approaches as well as the needed underlying project pipelines and capacities to attract such capital flows. In addition, orienting infrastructure investments to be green, inclusive, and job creating, will also require accompanying policy and regulatory support. This support should include globally acceptable green project selection frameworks, policies to phase out fossil fuel subsidies, carbon pricing, and reforming procurement programs and value chains.

B. Sizing the Green Finance Market

Targeting green pools of PIC capital for green infrastructure investments in ASEAN countries can address many of the critical factors noted above. Global pools of capital are available on the scales needed for meeting financing gaps as noted above but increasingly look for the "green" category of investments.

The market size. Based on estimates by the Global Sustainable Investment Review, which collates trends on sustainable investments in local sustainable investment forums across Europe, the United States, Canada, Japan, Australia, and New Zealand, global assets within the sustainable investment universe stood at $30.7 trillion at the beginning of 2018, a 34% increase over the previous 2 years.[36] The study also showed rising interest across the world from retail and institutional investors in using a sustainable and environmental, social, and governance lens for making investments.

In the Southeast Asia region, estimates by the Development Bank of Singapore (DBS) and the UN Environment Inquiry indicate the "green finance opportunity" in ASEAN (before COVID-19) to be $3 trillion (2016–2030) from four sectors: infrastructure; renewable energy; energy efficiency; and food, agriculture, and land use.[37]

Multilaterals. IFIs have also identified funding availability for climate and green infrastructure. ADB was the first MDB to make a climate finance commitment at the United Nations Climate Change Summit in 2015 setting a target of doubling its annual climate investments from $3 billion to $6 billion per year by the end of 2020. As evidence of the growing green finance market for infrastructure in the region, ADB already achieved that target a year ahead of schedule and is pursuing an ambitious target for climate-related investments to reach a cumulative $80 billion (2019–2030) under its *Strategy 2030* with a commitment to make 75% of all ADB projects climate relevant by 2030.[38]

The Amundi Planet Emerging Green One fund jointly promoted by the International Finance Corporation (IFC) and Amundi Asset Management, another example of an IFI-enabled vehicle, raised over $1.4 billion for investment, with IFC having identified an opportunity as large as $29 trillion in emerging markets to be funded by both green and non-green bonds.[39]

ADB's Action Plan for Healthy Oceans and Sustainable Blue Economies for Asia and the Pacific also provides an indication of the size of financing needs, as well as available funds for a specific thematic area within the overall green finance envelope. The plan aims to expand ADB financing and technical assistance for ocean health and marine economy projects to $5 billion from 2019 to 2024, including cofinancing from partners.[40] It will focus on four areas: (i) creating inclusive livelihoods and business opportunities in sustainable tourism and fisheries, (ii) protecting and restoring coastal and marine ecosystems and key rivers, (iii) reducing land-based sources of marine pollution, and (iv) improving sustainability in port and coastal infrastructure development.

---

[36] Global Sustainable Investment Alliance. 2018. *2018 Global Sustainable Investment Review*.
[37] UNEP and DBS. 2017. *Green Finance Opportunities in ASEAN*.
[38] ADB. 2018. *Strategy 2030: Achieving a Prosperous, Inclusive, Resilient, and Sustainable Asia and the Pacific*. Manila. July.
[39] Imperial College. 2020. Converting Emerging Markets to Green Finance: Amundi and the IFC. March.
[40] ADB. 2019. *Action Plan for Healthy Oceans and Sustainable Blue Economies*. Manila. May.

Size of the green bonds market. Green bonds, often seen as a proxy for the size of the green finance market, have seen massive growth in the last 4 years and more recently are giving rise to various thematic instruments such as sustainability bonds, social bonds, sustainability-linked bonds, green loans, and sustainable loans. Figure 4 outlines the growth trajectory of the market, with a remarkable jump of 78% in 2018–2019.

Figure 4: Growth of the Green Finance Market

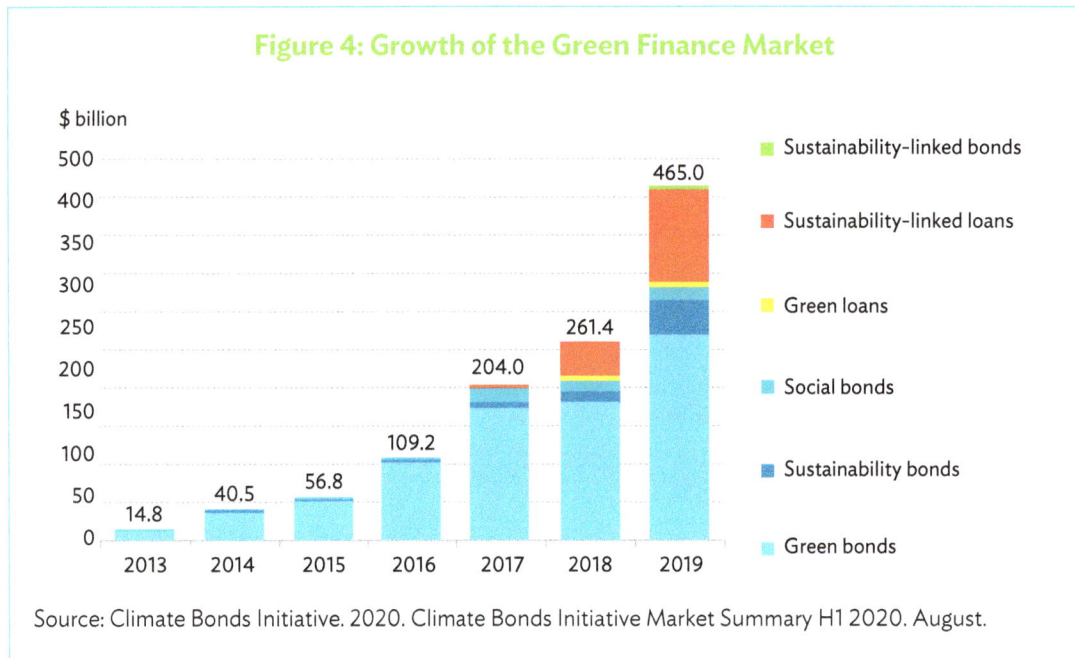

Source: Climate Bonds Initiative. 2020. Climate Bonds Initiative Market Summary H1 2020. August.

> *We believe that sustainability, and climate change in particular, are reshaping the investment management industry. As part of this, we are exiting investments that carry high environmental, social, and governance risks and we have an ambitious plan to grow our sustainable funds under management to about $1 trillion by the end of the decade. We believe that climate-integrated portfolios can provide better risk-adjusted returns on our investment to our investors over the long term.*
>
> *We have a lot of demand for green bonds from our clients for issuance. Our problem is not demand, it's supply. This is fantastic news for ASEAN issuers. There are takeaways. There is an incredibly strong demand from clients, on allocating capital to sustainable investments and labelled green bonds in particular. Tapping this source of funding for potential issuers needs that you can diversify your investor base; it means you can increase the resiliency of bond performance through volatile markets, and it can help you fund beneficial projects that you need to do anyway. This shift toward a greater availability of sustainable financing is going to be here for many years to come. During the pandemic, we have actually seen a reacceleration of these sustainable investment flows. We think that sustainability and growth actually go hand in hand.*
>
> **Venn Saltirov, Director Asia Pacific Fixed Income, BlackRock. ADB-CBI Webinar on Green Finance and Capital Markets Approaches for Post COVID-19 Economic Recovery, 9 July 2020.**

The Climate Bonds Initiative (CBI) estimates the volume of green bond and loan issuance globally at $258 billion in 2019, an increase of over 50% from 2018. In the ASEAN region, the issuance of green bonds and green loans almost doubled in 2019, reaching $8.1 billion.[41] This reflects the strong appetite from global investors in the green investment space.

C. Green Frameworks for Global Green Finance

One key aspect of attracting global flows of green capital is the acceptability and credibility of the "green" label on such infrastructure opportunities. Globally aligned green frameworks with sector taxonomies and eligibility principles will be key to this, so as to avoid projects, companies, or countries being seen as greenwashing or purpose-washing. Significant progress has been made globally in developing such green frameworks and standards and include the following:

- The Green Bond Principles and recently the Social Bond Principles and Sustainability Bond Principles have become the leading global framework for the issuance of green, social and sustainability bonds for which the International Capital Market Association (ICMA) serves as secretariat.[42]

- The Climate Bonds Standards and Certification scheme, a labelling scheme for bonds and loans, is used to prioritize investments that genuinely contribute to addressing climate change.[43]

- The ASEAN Green Bond Standards and recently the ASEAN Social Bond Standards and the ASEAN Sustainability Bond Standards were developed to align with ICMA's Green and Social Bond Principles, and Sustainability Bond Guidelines.[44]

- The EU adopted in June 2020 the Taxonomy Regulation, a key piece of legislation that will contribute to the European Green Deal by boosting private sector investment in green and sustainable projects. It will help create the world's first-ever "green list," a classification system for sustainable economic activities, that will create a common language that investors can use everywhere when investing in projects and economic activities that have a substantial positive impact on the climate and the environment. By enabling investors to reorient investments toward more sustainable technologies and businesses, this piece of legislation will be instrumental for the EU to become climate neutral by 2050.[45]

- In the loan market space, the Loan Market Association (LMA) and the Asia Pacific Loan Market Association have issued the Green Loan Principles as a benchmark for the wholesale green loan market, and also the Sustainability Linked Loan Principles.[46]

---

[41] CBI. 2020. The ASEAN Green Finance State of the Market 2019.
[42] International Capital Market Association. Green, Social, and Sustainability Bonds.
[43] CBI. 2019. *Climate Bonds Standard Version 3.0*. December.
[44] ASEAN Capital Markets Forum. Initiatives. Sustainable Finance. Development of a Sustainable Asset Class in ASEAN.
[45] European Commission. 2020. Sustainable Finance: Commission welcomes the adoption by the European Parliament of the Taxonomy Regulation. 18 June.
[46] LMA. 2018. *Green Loan Principles*. United Kingdom. December; and LMA. 2019. *Sustainability Linked Loan Principles. United Kingdom*. March.

ASEAN Catalytic Green Finance Facility Principles. The ACGF, managed by ADB, has also developed a set of Investment Principles and Eligibility Criteria for selecting projects for financing.[47] The principles include a taxonomy of eligible sectors and green indicators for setting targets, which include both a reduction in GHG emissions and other environmental indicators. The ACGF principles were aligned with the Joint MDBs-International Development Finance Club Common Principles for Climate Mitigation Finance Tracking and can provide a framework for identifying green recovery investments. Eligible sectors in the taxonomy include renewable energy; lower carbon and efficient energy generation; energy efficiency; agriculture, forestry and land use; non-energy GHG reductions; waste and wastewater; and transport.

---

[47] ACGF. 2020. *Investment Principles and Eligibility Criteria*. April.

3 GREEN RECOVERY PACKAGES AND FINANCE MECHANISMS: EXAMPLES

Drilling station and well testing station at Supreme Energy, Muara Laboh project, West Sumatera, Indonesia.
(photo by Gerhard Joren/ADB)

A number of countries have begun to develop economic packages or strategies to recover from the impacts of COVID-19 and several of these have a pointedly green focus. Examples of green finance mechanisms and instruments that have been used to catalyze green finance flows have also already been seen in some countries pre-COVID-19. These recent green recovery packages, as well as existing green finance mechanisms and instruments, can be useful to countries in the ASEAN region in developing their own green recovery packages and are noted in this chapter.

A. Green Recovery Packages

Several countries, especially in Europe, have announced recovery packages and approaches for specific sectors, which include a green, climate, or sustainability focus. Some of these examples are included below and could be useful tools for policymakers in the ASEAN region when compiling their own green finance strategies (see Box 3 and Infographic on p. 24).

Germany's Green Recovery Stimulus

In June 2020, Germany proposed one of the largest green stimulus packages thus far, with a massive €130 billion stimulus "future package" featuring at least €50 billion for climate-related spending.[48] This includes plans to boost electric vehicle sales, improve building energy efficiency, enhance public transport networks, develop hydrogen infrastructure, and shift the cost of renewables subsidies onto general taxation. Subsidies for electric vehicles were doubled. Proposed measures include supporting a green recovery in municipalities, for example, through installing low-carbon energy and heat systems in public buildings. The focus on green measures comes alongside plans to reduce value added tax from 19% to 16% for 6 months starting 1 July 2020, to increase loans for small businesses, and increase investment in R&D and digital infrastructure.

The European Green Deal

In response to a November 2019 declaration of a climate emergency by the European Parliament, the European Commission proposed a Green Deal for limiting global warming and ensuring that GHG emissions are significantly reduced. The European Green Deal aims to transform many aspects of its members' economies and has received renewed support from its 27 member countries post-COVID-19.[49]

Described by European Commission President Ursula von der Leyen as "Europe's man on the moon moment," the 27 member states of the EU created a plan to achieve net carbon neutrality by 2050 by overhauling transportation, construction, agriculture, and energy.[50] As noted by EU Vice-President Frans Timmermans on road maps for the recovery, "We can do it in two ways. We can repeat what we did before and throw a lot of money to the old economy, or we can be smart and combine this with the necessity to move to a green economy. I think this is a huge opportunity. In the European Union, we see the Green Deal as our growth strategy."[51]

Working through a regulatory and legislative framework, the green deal will aim to set clear overarching targets; a bloc-wide goal of net zero carbon emissions by 2050, and a 50%–55% cut in emissions by 2030 (compared with 1990 levels). There will also be incentives to encourage private sector investment, with action plans for key sectors and goals such as halting species loss, cutting waste, and better use of natural resources. Focusing on all EU budgetary spending to be made beneficial to the environment, science, research, and development, budgets

48   E. Kelly. 2020. *Germany Unveils €50B Stimulus for "Future-Focused" Technologies*. Science Business.
49   European Commission. 2019. Communication from the European Commission to the European Parliament, the European Council, the Council, the European Economic and Social Committee and the Committee of the Regions. The European Green Deal. Brussels. 11 December.
50   M. Mace. 2019. Europe's "Man on the Moon Moment:" Green Deal to Create World's First Climate-Neutral Continent. Edie.net. 11 December.
51   European Commission. 2020. Frans Timmermans' opening remarks at the Petersberg Climate Dialogue. 28 April.

will become more low-carbon oriented, and there will be a detailed road map of "50 actions for 2050" for other sectors. Jobs are expected to be created in new high-tech industries such as renewable energy, electric vehicle manufacturing, and sustainable building (footnote 49).

The Green Deal aims to catalyze at least €1 trillion into green investments, with the biggest share, €503 billion, from the EU budget which should lead to unlocking contributions of €114 billion from national governments, as well as €279 billion from the private sector. Additionally, a Just Transition Mechanism (JTM) has also been created.

a. **The Just Transition Mechanism.** The European Green Deal above also crucially includes a JTM, aimed at mobilizing at least €100 billion over the period 2021–2027 to provide financial support and technical assistance to help people, businesses, and regions that are most affected by the move toward a climate neutral economy. With core funds of €40 billion in the fund itself (provided primarily as grants), it will back productive investments in small and medium-sized enterprises, creation of new firms, research and innovation, environmental rehabilitation, clean energy, reskilling of workers, and job-search assistance. It will also include the transformation of existing carbon-intensive installations where these investments lead to substantial emission cuts and job protection. To access funds from the Just Transition Fund (JTF), EU countries will have to provide matching financing from various budgets. Extrapolated over 10 years, the Just Transition Mechanism will mobilize around €143 billion.[52]

b. **Leveraged public sector loan facility.** Another pillar created under the JTM, the European Investment Bank (EIB) public sector loan facility, with contributions from the EU budget of €1.5 billion, will enable the EIB to lend €10 billion, which in turn is expected to mobilize €25 billion to €30 billion of public investments to support just transition objectives over the period 2021–2027. These loans would provide public sector entities with resources to implement measures to facilitate the transition to climate neutrality, such as energy and transport infrastructure, district heating networks, and energy efficiency measures including renovation of buildings, as well as social infrastructure (footnote 51).

c. **Recovery Fund for Europe - "Next Generation EU."** On 21 July 2020, EU leaders agreed on a recovery plan for mitigating COVID 19's Impacts. Keeping the Green Deal at its core for engineering a more sustainable Europe, the recovery plan includes two responses: (i) a €750 billion "Next Generation EU" recovery fund, and (ii) a reinforced long-term budget for the EU for 2021–2027 of €1.1 trillion.[53]

The Next Generation EU fund will raise new financing from the capital markets of up to €750 billion on behalf of the EU. About €390 billion of this fund will then be available to be distributed as grants, with the remaining €360 billion disbursed as loans to fund recovery in members states. A core component of the grants portion, about €312 billion, will be provided to member states through a Recovery and Resilience Facility, one of seven programs created to manage the funds raised, including a Rural Development Fund and support to the JTF.

In order to access these funds, member states will have to prepare national recovery and resilience plans for 2021–2023 in accordance with country-specific recommendations and the road map for green and digital transitions. The disbursement of grants will take place only if the agreed milestones and targets set out in the recovery and resilience plans are fulfilled. The EU sustainable finance taxonomy will also be applied to filter investments into technologies that contribute to at least one of six defined environmental objectives, such as climate change mitigation, with a "do no harm" principle.

---

[52] European Commission. 2020. The European Green Deal Investment Plan and Just Transition Mechanism Explained. 14 January.
[53] European Council. 2020. A Recovery Plan for Europe. July.

The Republic of Korea's New Green Deal

The Republic of Korea is aiming for net zero emissions by 2050 and an end to coal financing. The plan includes large-scale investments in renewable energy, the introduction of a carbon tax, the phaseout of domestic and overseas coal financing by public institutions, and the creation of a Regional Energy Transition Centre to support workers' transition to green jobs.[54]

New Zealand's Focus on Environment and Jobs

In New Zealand's budget for 2020, $1.1 billion has been set aside to create 11,000 environment jobs across the country. This includes a new $200 million fund to create jobs restoring wetlands, regenerating planting, nature-based tourism jobs, and enhancing biodiversity on public and private lands.[55]

Aviation Recovery Packages

Notable among the recovery packages has been the focus on aviation and the use of conditional recapitalization and bailouts to airline companies to encourage a reduction in emissions and short haul flights (see Infographic on page 24).The Government of the United Kingdom announced a Jet-Zero strategy with a view to reducing emissions as part of their net zero carbon emission target within a generation and has set up a Jet-Zero Council. This is expected to be a feature of recovery strategies in keeping with a just transition and ensuring "brown to green" trajectories are triggered, even if in the short-term some traditionally "brown" sectors such as airlines are recipients of support, however complemented by measures that ensure fossil fuel are not embedded in long-term plans.

Box 3: Emerging Policy Suggestions for a Green Recovery

A number of high-level dialogues and think tanks have emphasized the need for a green recovery as noted below:

The Petersberg Climate Dialogue, April 2020. This key gathering of speakers including Kristalina Georgieva of the International Monetary Fund, Mark Carney (United Nations [UN] Special Envoy for Climate Action and Finance) and Lord Stern (Chair of the Grantham Research Institute on Climate Change and the Environment at the London School of Economics and Political Science, and adviser to the 26th UN Climate Change Conference [COP26]), senior officials and ministers from Germany and the United Kingdom, and private sector funds identified the following key themes for recovery strategies:

- **Build back better.** Climate change and environment considerations must be front and center in coronavirus disease (COVID-19) responses.
- **Centrality of international financial institutions.** Multilateral development banks play a key role in providing or crowding in of capital.
- **Conditional aid to the private sector.** Aid must be linked to clear green impacts, which will result in gaining a broad consensus.
- **Financing the recovery.** Financing will be done through various green finance instruments such as green bonds, public funds, carbon pricing, etc.

continued on next page

---

[54] C. Farand. 2020. South Korea to Implement Green New Deal after Ruling Party Election Win. Climate Home News. 16 April.
[55] Government of New Zealand, Department of Conservation. 2020. $1.1 Billion Investment to Create 11,000 Environment Jobs in Our Regions.

Box 3 *continued*

Infrastructure Asia-ADB High-Level Panel Discussions, May 2020. A high-level panel of private sector entities hosted by the Asian Development Bank (ADB) and Singapore's Infrastructure Asia discussed possible recovery strategies for catalyzing capital into clean energy across Southeast Asia. Key themes emerging included suggestions for governments and ADB to help create de-risking instruments that could help attract capital including regional green financing platforms, completion guarantees, and first loss structures for green bonds.

"Greener After" Policy Paper, May 2020, Jacques Delors Institute. This policy paper calls for a "very large green investment plan" that "delivers the necessary economic stimulus and builds resilience to future shocks." The paper recommends green investments as critical for recovery, as these investments are timely, temporary, and targeted measures able to stimulate the economy quickly until it recovers and can accelerate the structural transformation of an economy toward a more healthy and resilient future, characterized by zero pollution, biodiversity restoration, and climate neutrality by 2050. The paper provides criteria for policy makers to use in prioritizing investments that can aid a green economic stimulus plan as well as concrete investment recommendations in five essential sectors: buildings, road mobility, clean innovation, circular economy, and coastal tourism. It calls for European Union member states to invest at least €800 billion in these over the next 5 years.

Other upcoming forums. Discussions are underway in several policy and international forums to address the emerging scenarios with a view to aligning economic recovery with a more sustainable and greener trajectory. Some of the prominent ones include:

- **COP26 (proposed for 2021 in Glasgow**). This calls for greater climate ambition and cooperation. Key themes include the transition to clean energy, clean transport, nature-based solutions, adaptation and resilience, and "bringing it all together, finance."
- **Finance in Common summit**. This will drive collaboration among public development banks in the COVID-19 context in linking short-term needs to long-term sustainable transformations and will meet at the Paris Peace Forum in November 2020. Outputs will be presented at the Group of Twenty (G20) and COP26. More information can be found at https://financeincommon.org/ .
- **Financing for Development Forum**. Following the Addis Ababa Action Agenda in 2015, it provides a global framework for financing sustainable development aligning all financial flows and policies with socioeconomic and environmental factors. Its core areas of international finance and development cooperation and elements of debt and debt sustainability will be key at a systemic level in the post-COVID-19 scenario. More details can be found at https://www.un.org/sustainabledevelopment/financing-for-development/.
- **High Level Political Forum**: A core United Nations platform for follow-up and review of the 2030 Agenda for Sustainable Development and the 17 Sustainable Development Goals, which are under the auspices of the Economic and Social Council will report to the United Nations General Assembly. Information is provided at https://sustainabledevelopment.un.org/hlpf.

Sources: Asian Development Bank; United Nations; P. Lamy et al. 2020. Greener After: A Green Recovery Stimulus for a Post-COVID-19 Europe. *Jacques Delors Institute Policy Paper 200514*; and Finance in Common.

Green Packages Among ASEAN Member States

Examples of existing packages in the region, including those initiated and developed pre-COVID-19, are outlined in this section and are highly relevant to build upon for a post-COVID-19 green recovery. It is crucial that new programs are also identified and developed in line with national plans that incorporate green, environment-friendly, and resilient principles.

a. **Green Program, Philippines.** This government program aims to provide ₱2.5 billion in assistance to make 145 cities more livable and sustainable. As part of "Build, Build, Build," the national infrastructure development program of the Government of the Philippines, this can be a vital component of green recovery packages targeting both green livability as well as investments in urban areas through scaling up projects such as EDSA Greenways that aim to provide non-motorized alternative for commuter travel.[56]

b. **"Build, Build, Build" Program, Philippines.** The government has maintained infrastructure as one of the government's priorities for the economic recovery under its $160 billion plan, which can be a major impetus to creating projects, investment opportunities, and green jobs.[57]

c. **Action Plan to Reduce Plastic Pollution, Indonesia.** This was unveiled in April 2020 by the multi-stakeholder National Plastic Action Partnership, led by the Government of Indonesia. The action plan calls for total capital investments of $5.1 billion to achieve its outlined systemic change scenario from 2017 to 2025 and lays out a road map for reducing plastic leakage in Indonesia's coastal waters by 70% by 2025 and near zero by 2040 through a circular economy approach.[58] The program can have a society-wide and long-lasting green economic impact with investments likely to flow into green small and medium-sized enterprises and sustainable infrastructure for recycling, new technologies for packaging and recycling, along with waste disposal facilities.

d. **National Economic Recovery Program, Indonesia.** Launched in May 2020, this provides the latest stimulus policies for the economy in a program estimated to cost $43 billion and comprising of tax breaks for industries, capital injections into state-owned enterprises (SOEs), and liquidity support for the banking industry, among others. Indonesia had already been working on green bonds and sukuk bonds (Islamic bond) issuance pre-COVID-19 as well as creating a Sustainable Development Goals platform under the government financing institution PT Sarana Multi Infrastruktur (PT SMI). These programs might be further leveraged for green recovery plans.[59]

e. **Thailand.** Thailand expects its ongoing investment in major infrastructure to be the basis of growth in the next 5 years, with a plan for 92 PPP projects worth B1.09 trillion ($33.39 billion) from 2020 to 2027.[60] Thailand has also embarked on the issuance of sovereign sustainability bonds to fund green infrastructure projects as seen in August 2020.

f. **Malaysia.** Malaysia supports an ASEAN economic recovery plan to ensure critical infrastructure for trade and trading routes via air, land and sea are secured. An allocation worth $450 million has been made from the national budget to implement small infrastructure projects, including $33 million for maintenance of alternative electricity and water supply in rural areas, maintaining roads, bridges, streetlights, drainage systems, and water supplies, at the federal, state, and local levels to assist small contractors and encourage

---

56 Government of the Philippines, Department of Budget and Management. 2018. Green, Green, Green Pushes City Governments to Build Better Open Spaces. 27 June.

57 ABS-CBN News. 2020. "Build Build Build" A priority as Philippines Resets from Pandemic: NEDA Chief. 30 April.

58 World Economic Forum. 2020. *Radically Reducing Plastic Pollution in Indonesia: A Multistakeholder Action Plan National Plastic Action Partnership*. April.

59 ASEAN Briefing. 2020. Indonesia Launches National Economic Recovery Program.

60 O. Sriring. 2020. Thailand Plans $33 Billion Public–Private Investment Projects. *Reuters*. 15 April..

economic activities. It also plans to manage the tender process for a 1,400-megawatt solar power project, expected to generate $1.1 billion in investments.[61]

g.   **National Strategy on Green Growth, Viet Nam.** The centerpiece of the Government of Viet Nam's efforts to stem environmental degradation, this strategy will provide a strong framework especially through the development of investment guidelines and methodologies for prioritizing investment opportunities and mobilizing public and private finance for green economic recovery projects.[62]

h.   **National Strategic Plan on Green Growth, Cambodia.** The plan was prepared to propel Cambodia toward a green economy focusing on efficient use of natural resources, environmental sustainability, green jobs, green technology, and economic reform. It prioritizes green incentives for catalyzing investments, including green taxes, green finance, green credit, and green microfinance.[63]

---

[61]   ASEAN Briefing. 2020. Malaysia Issues Stimulus Package to Combat COVID-19 Impact.

[62]   Climate & Development Knowledge Network. 2013. Vietnam's National Green Growth Strategy. April.

[63]   Government of Cambodia, National Council on Green Growth. 2013. National Strategic Plan on Green Growth 2013–2030.

RESPONSES TO POST-COVID-19
GREEN RECOVERY

REGIONAL AND NATIONAL STIMULUS PACKAGES

EUROPEAN UNION

€750 billion ($847 billion)

Next Generation EU recovery fund and Just Transition Fund for climate action.

GERMANY

€130 billion stimulus package

Promoting electric vehicles, public transport, clean technology, and greening buildings.

NORWAY

NOK 3.6 billion ($370 million)

Support for hydrogen and battery technology, offshore wind, and green shipping.

REPUBLIC OF KOREA

W76 trillion ($62 billion)

Digital New Deal and a Green New Deal to boost job creation.

INDONESIA

$3 billion for SDG Indonesia One plus resources for other initiatives.

Green financing facility and reducing plastic pollution in rivers and coast.

PHILIPPINES

₱2.5 billion ($50 million)

Support to make 145 cities more livable and sustainable.

CO$_2$

VIET NAM

Mobilizing public and private finance for green, resilient growth.

UNITED KINGDOM

£40 million ($50.54 million)
£283 million ($357.57 million)

Clean Growth Fund and transport subsidies to drive a green recovery.

LUXEMBOURG

UP TO €30,000/HOUSEHOLD ($33,800) AND €8,000/ELECTRIC CAR ($9,017)

Subsidies for households, public transport, and electric vehicles.

NOTE: The Asian Development Bank is not responsible for any information gathered here from publicly available sources and subject to change. Data from June 2020.

A green recovery is key to ensuring a sustainable and resilient return to growth and development after COVID-19. Global examples show how climate change and other green themes can be central to COVID-19 responses so that countries can build back better.

AIRLINES STIMULI

Air France will receive €7 billion ($7.5 billion), including €4 billion in bank loans guaranteed by the state and a €3 billion loan direct from the state, subject to presenting a plan for reducing CO_2 emissions.

Austrian Airlines will receive €600 million ($667 million), including €150 million in direct state aid, €300 million from commercial bank loans (with state guarantees for 90%), and €150 million in equity from Lufthansa. The aid package is conditional on reducing its domestic and global CO_2 emissions by 50% and 30% respectively by 2030.

The Government of Sweden is planning to invest up to $537 million into the **Scandinavian airline SAS** as part of a drastic recapitalization plan, which may be subject to the airline meeting criteria on lower emissions to better align itself with the 1.5-degree target of the Paris Agreement on climate change.

KLM Royal Dutch Airlines, could receive €2 billion—4 billion **state support** if it presents a plan for 50% emission cuts by 2030 and 50% on domestic flights by 2024.

EU transport and infrastructure ministers have agreed to make **international train transport** more attractive than short haul flights.

POLICY RECOMMENDATIONS

Greener After | Jacques Delors Institute.
Five areas for a green recovery: buildings, road mobility, clean innovation, the circular economy, and coastal tourism

Stimulus actions for a greener and more resilient property sector | UK's Green Finance Institute.
The UK's economic recovery should contribute to its green targets and include stimulating consumer demand, scaling up the retrofit supply chain and building low-carbon buildings.

Wellbeing Economics for the COVID-19 recovery | The Wellbeing Economy Alliance.
10 principles to "Build Back Better": **1**. Ecologically safe and environmentally just goals, **2**. Protecting environmental standards, **3**. Green infrastructure, **4**. Universal basic services, **5**. Guaranteed livelihoods, **6**. Fair distribution, **7**. Better democracy, **8**. Wellbeing economics organizations, **9**. Cooperation, **10**. Public control of money

How a post-pandemic stimulus can both create jobs and help the climate | McKinsey.
Post-COVID-19 recovery should be green, should create jobs, and achieve climate change targets. McKinsey estimates that investing €75 billion – €150 billion in a green recovery plan could create €180 billion–€350 billion in added value, up to three million new jobs, and reduce carbon emissions by 15–30% by 2030.

WHO manifesto for a healthy and green COVID-19 recovery | World Health Organization (WHO)
Six principles for a healthy and green recovery:
1. Protect and preserve nature, the source of human health;
2. Invest in water, sanitation, clean energy, and health care;
3. Ensure a speedy energy transition; **4**. Promote healthy, sustainable food systems; **5**. Build healthy, livable cities;
6. Stop using taxpayers money to fund pollution

Central Banks | Andrew Bailey (Bank of England), Francois Villeroy de Galhau (Banque de France) and Frank Elderson (Chair of the Network for Green-ing the Financial System)
The COVID-19 pandemic offers a chance to green the global economy if we change the way we live, work, and travel. Financial support should contain climate-related conditions.

About the ASEAN Catalytic Green Finance Facility
The ACGF is an innovative finance facility under the ASEAN Infrastructure Fund dedicated to accelerating green infrastructure investments in Southeast Asia. It supports ASEAN governments to prepare and source public and private financing for infrastructure projects that promote environmental sustainability and contribute to climate change goals. The ACGF is owned by the 10 ASEAN member states and the Asian Development Bank, which also administers the facility.

ACGF | ADB

B. Capital Markets Instruments

1. Green and Sustainability Bonds

Any green finance recovery strategy should consider the use of capital markets to raise funds from global investors. Before COVID-19, global green bond markets had been growing rapidly, with increasing investor focus on environmental, social and governance (ESG) factors. Sustainable investing assets reached $30.7 trillion at the start of 2018, a growth of 34% in 2 years in the five major markets of the United States, Europe, Japan, Canada, and Australia and New Zealand.[64] With the Action Plan on Sustainable Finance mobilizing the capital markets toward green investments and the recent ratification of the Sustainable Finance taxonomy at the EU Parliament, momentum can be expected to only grow further. The Climate Bonds Initiative (CBI) estimates that the volume of green bond and loan issuance globally reached $258 billion in 2019, an increase of over 50% from $171 billion in 2018, due to strong investor and issuer interest (Figure 5).

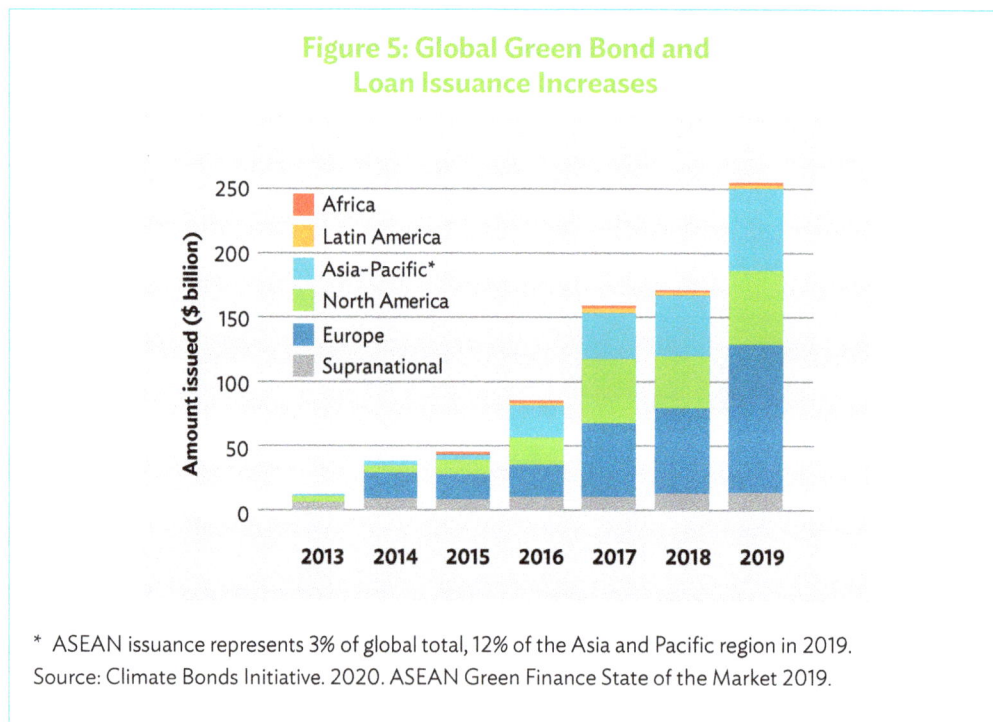

Figure 5: Global Green Bond and Loan Issuance Increases

* ASEAN issuance represents 3% of global total, 12% of the Asia and Pacific region in 2019.
Source: Climate Bonds Initiative. 2020. ASEAN Green Finance State of the Market 2019.

In the ASEAN region, the issuance of green bonds and green loans had almost doubled in 2019 from the previous year, reaching $8.1 billion.[65] The ASEAN region has shown significant growth in the green debt market with a cumulative issuance of $13.4 billion at the end of 2019, with varying growth among individual countries (Figure 6).

---

[64] Global Sustainable Investment Alliance. 2018. *2018 Global Sustainable Investment Review*.

[65] CBI. 2020. *The ASEAN Green Finance State of the Market 2019*.

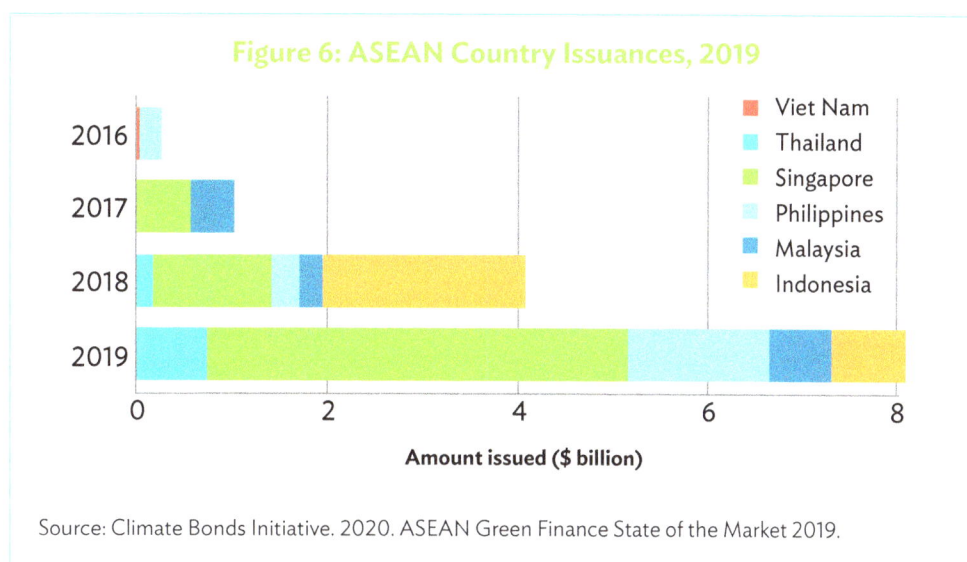

Figure 6: ASEAN Country Issuances, 2019

Source: Climate Bonds Initiative. 2020. ASEAN Green Finance State of the Market 2019.

A mechanism to deepen. Despite these trends, when viewed in the context of wider global and regional trends, ASEAN region issuances represent only 3% of the global total and 12% of the Asia and Pacific region total in 2019. Deepening the green bond market in the region, especially exploring the opportunity for issuances by SOEs, local governments, and special purpose vehicles for utilities is a massive opportunity. However, there remain inherent challenges around credit ratings and capacities and so governments need to create enabling frameworks to grow this area further, which can be a source of much greater flows of capital for each country.

2. Transition Bonds: Brown to Green

In 2019, this new instrument emerged, with at least three issuances of transition bonds and their accompanying instrument receiving much attention from investors. Transition bonds are different from green bonds, which are designed for green industries alone, i.e., industries in those sectors defined in green taxonomies that are already on the road to reducing GHG emissions, with renewable energy being the most common example.

Transition bonds are a new asset class targeted at "brown" industries with high GHG emissions, which have a clear and explicit goal of becoming less brown or greener. These industries include oil, mining, agriculture, and heavy industry (e.g., cement, iron, steel).

Accessing the capital markets has been a challenge for brown industries. But given their very high impact on GHG emissions, any effort to reduce these impacts should be encouraged and transition bonds have emerged as a response to this need. Evidently, transition bonds need very clear GHG reduction metrics and targets as well as transparent monitoring under identified "go greener" projects. For example, an energy company could finance its efforts to capture and store carbon emissions or commence new renewable energy projects using such transition bonds.

The Marfrig Transition Bond, 2019

Marfrig, the world's second largest beef company in terms of capacity, raised **$500 million** through a transition bond arranged by BNP Paribas, ING Groep NV, and Banco Santander SA.

The proceeds of the bond will be used to purchase cattle from ranchers who comply with non-deforestation and other sustainable criteria such as animal welfare and fair labor practices.

An example of a bond (the Marfrig Transition Bond) in the food industry shows the potential for impact.[66] The meat industry has been noted for its high carbon footprint through methane emitted by cows as well as cattle ranching that increase deforestation and reduce carbon sinks. A 2013 study by the Food and Agriculture Organization of the United Nations (FAO) conservatively estimated total annual emissions from animal agriculture (production emissions plus land use change) to be about 14.5% of all human emissions, of which beef contributed 41%.[67] The World Resources Institute (WRI) further projected beef-related emissions to grow by over 88% between 2010 and 2050, and pasture to expand by roughly 400 million hectares, putting the global goal of limiting temperature rise to 1.5 to 2 degrees Celsius out of reach.[68] Such bonds could also help companies create strong brown to green metrics such as improving farming practices of suppliers, better supply traceability systems, improving water usage, etc.[69] This would focus attention on the overall behavior of an issuer rather than solely focusing on use of proceeds or existing issuer profile as in the case of green bonds. Given the scale of the need to urgently reduce GHG emissions from existing brown industries, transition bonds could hasten the shift in such industries while also expanding the green credit market significantly, which is still only a fraction of the overall financing need.

C. Green Finance Catalytic Mechanisms: De-risking Projects

Green infrastructure projects in developing countries often have a higher risk due to a host of reasons—new technology, higher capital cost, higher operating expenses, and higher construction risk—and may not pass the standard risk appraisal processes of commercial banks. In such cases, projects may be unable to attract or service commercial debt, due to their higher pricing and shorter tenors. To make such projects bankable, and attract commercial financiers and achieve financial closure, specific de-risking support may need to be provided. The need for such catalytic mechanisms is even greater now, in the post-COVID-19 environment with a perception of higher risk in many infrastructure sectors in emerging markets. ADB and other development agencies have been helping developing countries create financing vehicles by providing the financial structuring expertise and concessional funds required to de-risk projects and incentivize private sector investments. Some mechanisms and instruments are discussed below, with both regional and international examples.

1. Shandong Green Development Fund, People's Republic of China

The Shandong Green Development Fund (SGDF) is a transformational financing mechanism created with ADB support, aiming at leveraging $1.5 billion of funding to Shandong Province in the People's Republic of China (Figure 7).[70] The SGDF aims to blend funding from international financing institutions with private, institutional, and commercial finance for climate impacting subprojects. The subprojects must meet SGDF green framework criteria, aligned with the Green Climate Fund (GCF) investment framework.

The SGDF targets higher risk climate-resilient infrastructure subprojects, green and high technology manufacturing businesses, and investment in municipal and sectoral sub-funds in Shandong Province. All SGDF investments must follow the principles, terms, and conditions agreed and approved by ADB and SGDF cofinanciers. These include subproject eligibility criteria, governance, implementation arrangements, environmental and social management systems, gender considerations, monitoring and evaluation, and verification.

---

66 *Financial Times.* 2020. The "Transition" Bonds Bridging the Gap Between Green and Brown. 3 January; S. Belmiloud. 2019. Marfrig's Transition Bond: A Low-Carbon Transition or More of the Same. *The FAIRR Initiative.* 22 August.

67 FAO. 2013. *Tackling Climate Change Through Livestock: A Global Assessment of Emissions and Mitigation Opportunities.* Rome.

68 R. Waite, T. Searchinger, and J. Ranganathan. "6 Pressing Questions About Beef and Climate Change." WRI Blog. 8 April 2019.

69 S. Belmiloud. 2019. Marfrig's Transition Bond: A Low-Carbon Transition or More of the Same. *The FAIRR Initiative.* 22 August.

70 ADB. 2020. Catalyzing Climate Finance with the Shandong Green Development Fund. *ADB Briefs* No. 144. July.

Figure 7: Case Study of the Shandong Green Development Fund, 2019

Description. To establish a Green Development Fund in Shandong Province that will leverage public sector funds to accelerate a variety of climate subprojects and catalyze private capital to these.

Cost and Financing Plan. $1.5 billion project financed by ADB loan of $100.0 million; $84.5 million by AFD; $113.6 million by KFW; $100.0 million by GCF; $360 million from public sources, and $740 million from private investors.

Green Impact and Criteria. The Green Development Fund will apply GCF's Investment Framework and leverage transformational investments with strong climate benefits, aiming at reducing carbon dioxide emissions by 3.75 million tons per annum.

✓ First ADB and the PRC Catalytic Green Finance Facility, using a financial intermediary modality.

✓ First GCF approved project for the PRC.

✓ High climate impact through several projects to reduce emissions by 3.75 million tons per annum by 2027.

✓ Directly builds resilience for at least 3 million people.

✓ SGDF to invest 75% in climate mitigation projects; 25% in climate adaptation projects.

AFD = Agence Française de Développement; KfW = Kreditanstalt für Wiederaufbau; GCF = Green Climate Fund; PRC = People's Republic of China.

Source: Asian Development Bank.

The SGDF is a dedicated investment fund, managed by a fund management company to mobilize capital at fund, sub-fund, as well as subproject levels from public and private sources. The fund finances a portion of the capital expenditure of selected climate subprojects for a capped period to make the subprojects bankable, by addressing upfront risks, and by promoting advanced technologies and an integrated approach to climate finance and infrastructure development.

2. Climate Finance Facility, Development Bank of South Africa

The Climate Finance Facility (CFF) at the Development Bank of Southern Africa (DBSA) is the first private sector climate finance facility in Africa using a pioneering green bank model. It aims to de-risk climate-friendly infrastructure projects and improve their bankability to attract private sector investment. Its successful implementation provides a model for replication in other developing countries. Established in 2019 jointly between DBSA and the GCF, it has a $110 million fund, with equal contributions from both.[71]

Target Leverage: $5 of private investment for each dollar directly invested.

Expected Impact: Avoidance of around 30 million tons of carbon dioxide equivalent during the lifetime of program; save around 23,000 jobs through water systems installation, over 400,000 indirect beneficiaries.

The CFF will use financial tools such as long-term subordinated debt and credit enhancements, subordinated debt, and tenor extensions to catalyze investment for projects that mitigate climate change. The facility aims to address market constraints and play a catalytic role with a blended finance approach to increase climate-related investments in Namibia, Lesotho, and Eswatini.

The DBSA's CFF will deliver outcomes related to GCF's Investment Criteria. Eligible sectors and subsectors for climate change mitigation and adaptation include renewable energy, energy efficiency, waste-to-energy, wastewater treatment, water efficiency, and sustainable transport. The minimum contribution from the CFF

---

[71] Convergence. 2019. Case Study: Climate Finance Facility. *Green Bank Network*. June.

is R50 million ($3 million). The CFF will support commercially viable projects, and a rigorous set of investment criteria will be followed for all potential investments considering economic, environmental, social, and technical aspects of the proposal.

3. ASEAN Catalytic Green Finance Facility

The ACGF is a green infrastructure financing facility under the ASEAN Infrastructure Fund (AIF), with funding commitments from several global development partners including ADB, the EIB, Agence Française de Développement (AFD), Kreditanstalt für Wiederaufbau (KfW), the Republic of Korea and the EU. This innovative initiative was launched in 2019 to accelerate the development of green infrastructure projects across Southeast Asia in support of ASEAN members' climate change and environmental sustainability goals. The ACGF uses a de-risking approach in the use of its funds— around $1.4 billion funding commitments from the AIF as well as ADB and other development partners—to bridge the funding gap and create bankable green infrastructure projects that can catalyze private capital, technologies, and management efficiencies. The ACGF, using AIF equity funds, currently offers a two-step sovereign guaranteed loan, designed with a lower rate of interest in the first 7 years and a step-up to a higher interest rate after the eighth year. This can be blended with funds committed by other ACGF partners, to the benefit of projects. This is in line with the principle of de-risking the most significant period of a project, namely construction and initial operations.

Project Eligibility: Projects supported must

- Be "Green" - per the ACGF Green Framework
- Be "Bankable" - the ACGF team will help structure
- Have a roadmap for private capital flow - the ACGF will help structure
- Have a sovereign guarantee for ACGF Funds.

ACGF Funds aim to leverage each $1 of public funds to attract at least $3 of commercial funds to projects

4. SDG Indonesia One - Green Finance Facility

Indonesia launched SDG Indonesia One in October 2018, as one of the first such SDG financing platforms across the world. With commitments from over 30 partners for almost $3 billion in funding, SDG Indonesia One can have a critical impact on sustainable investments into the country.[72]

ADB has been working with PT SMI, the national financial intermediary and the implementing agency for SDG Indonesia One to create a specific green finance facility under the platform. It aims to combine four principles: (i) support green or SDG-related infrastructure, (ii) provide a de-risking financing mechanism through innovative use of public funds, (iii) leverage commercial funds into projects with a 1x3 multiplier on average, and (iv) help prepare and structure green projects and innovative finance instruments. The SDG Indonesia One - Green Finance Facility aims to offer innovative financial products to eligible green infrastructure projects (against green, financial, technical and environmental, and social safeguards criteria), based and aligned with the needs and cash flows of the projects. SDG Indonesia One itself also provides a model for replication since it combines various aspects of a blended finance vehicle: de-risking funds, equity, and project preparation.

---

[72] Government of Indonesia, PT Sarana Multi Infrastruktur. 2020. SDG Indonesia One.

5. Green Public–Private Partnerships, Cambodia Solar Park Project

The PPP mechanism can be a vital tool for catalyzing private capital for green infrastructure. A model structure that could be replicated is that of the Cambodia Solar Park Project (Figure 8). This combined support from government and ADB to part-finance, develop, and bid out a project in the solar energy sector, led to bidding in 2019 that attracted 26 bids, and the lowest solar tariff in the ASEAN region. The project had two components.

Solar park facility. The solar park facility, including a sub-station and transmission lines—to accommodate up to 100 megawatts (MW) of solar photovoltaic (PV) power generation—is being constructed by Electricité du Cambodge (EDC) using public sector funds, including an ADB sovereign loan.

Solar photovoltaic plants. The plants within the park will be developed, financed, constructed, operated, and maintained by a private sector entity. EDC will purchase the power under a power purchase agreement (PPA), with the tariff determined through a competitive PPP bidding process.

ADB is already building on the project approach to create a program for replication across the ASEAN region, entitled ASEAN Scaling Up Renewables + Storage (ASSURE). The auctions strategy used in this project along with the tariff structure will serve as a benchmark for future projects.

Figure 8: Case Study of the Cambodia Solar Park Project, 2019

Description. Supporting Cambodia build a 100 MW Solar Power Park through a PPP approach in Kampong Chhnang Province. ADB support for transmission lines and park infrastructure; PPP financing for generation.

Cost and Financing Plan. For the ADB project, cost of $27.7 million financed by ADB loan of $7.7 million; $11.0 million loan, and $3.0 million grant from Strategic Climate Fund; EDC and government the rest.

ADB PPP Support. To EDC for bidding of 60 megawatts solar PV capacity.

✓ **Both** Climate Adaptation and Mitigation impacts.

✓ Massive **green impact** contributing to the needed 150–300 MW new PV Capacity (2020–2030) to help country meet its emission reduction commitments under the Paris Agreement.

✓ **Bankable** project with a rate of return of 8.4% – attracted private capital interest.

✓ **Lowest ASEAN bid tariff** achieved of $0.39 cents per kWh by Prime Alternative Co. Ltd.

ADB = Asian Development Bank, ASEAN = Association of Southeast Asian Nations, EDC = Electricité du Cambodge, kWh = kilowatt-hour, MW = megawatt, PPP = public-private partnership, PV = photovoltaic.
Source: ADB.

6. Blending Finance through Domestic Financial Institutions, Clean Energy Finance Investment Programme, India

ADB's sovereign loan of $200 million (a first loan from a multitranche facility of $500 million) to support lending by the Indian Renewable Energy Development Agency (IREDA) in 2015 is an example of a blending structure that aimed to accelerate funds flows into renewable energy. Utilizing the presence and reach of IREDA (a government owned nonbank financial institution established to promote renewable energy investment in India) allowed this facility loan to impact on at least 10 projects.

With the aim of leveraging long-term ADB sovereign debt funds to catalyze private sector investments into renewable energy subprojects including wind, biomass, hydropower, solar, and cogeneration technologies, the program offered ADB funds to finance up to 50% of a subproject's cost and thus attract multiples of financing from other sources. The program expects to have leveraged an estimated $300 million in equity and other investments from subproject sponsors, and at least $200 million of additional debt funds for a total investment program of around $1 billion, translating into approximately 990 MW of additional renewable energy capacity.

7. Credit Enhanced Climate Bond, Tiwi and Makban Geothermal Project, Philippines

The Philippines' first green bonds certified under the Climate Bond Initiative's geothermal criteria as a single project bond, the Tiwi Makban Geothermal project was de-risked by ADB via a loan and a guarantee to AP Renewables to support a $225 million green bond in 2016. AP Renewables, a subsidiary of Manila-based Aboitiz Power, issued the bond to refinance a 676.9-megawatt geothermal project. Credit enhancement by ADB with risk participation via the Credit Guarantee Investment Facility (established by ASEAN+3 governments and ADB), helped reduce the cost of capital by driving pricing of the bond down a few basis points, due to the bank's AAA rating. The issuance won the Project Bond of the year award at the Environmental Finance Green Bonds Awards in April 2017.[73] This transaction shows the possibility for credit-enhanced climate bonds to be an attractive alternative to bank financing, which can mobilize cost-effective, long-term capital to meet the region's infrastructure needs.

Issuer: AP Renewables

Issued: February 2016

Tenor: 10 years

Credit guarantee: 75% of the principal and interest guaranteed by ADB

Loan amount: $37 million by ADB

External Review: Climate Bonds certification via DNV GL under the Geothermal criteria

Deal format: Private placement

---

[73] *Environmental Finance.* 2017. Project Bond of the Year - AP Renewables. 7 April

4 GREEN FINANCE CONCEPTS TO STIMULATE POST-COVID-19 RECOVERY

BTS skytrain pulls over to pick up passengers in Bangkok, Thailand. (photo by Zen Nuntawinyu/ADB)

Perhaps the possibility of rising sovereign debt is one of the biggest challenges facing governments in the COVID-19 era, itself arising from the need to spend on relief activities (mostly underway) and recovery activities (mostly yet to start). There is thus a real and critical need to catalyze funds from commercial, private, PPP, and capital market sources. With rising risk perceptions especially arising from at-threat revenue projections, governments have to create the right mechanisms and instruments that can perform this catalytic role of de-risking and attracting such capital. This is also an opportunity for governments to innovate and implement such financial instruments that help accelerate their commitments to climate change under the Paris Agreement and the Sustainable Development Goals (SDGs), and hence "build back better" as is being increasingly voiced across the world.

> *COVID-19 is the first global crisis where sustainable finance and responsible investment tools and mechanisms could make a real difference. Added to this, there is unmet investor demand for financial assets that incorporate Environmental, Social and Governance (ESG) factors.*
>
> **London School of Economics and Political Science**

During discussion while preparing this paper, a number of climate advisors and investors noted the clear signaling by investors, including pension funds in Europe, of their interest in governments, in Asia in general and Southeast Asia in particular, to create sustainable and green recovery plans that can lead to green bankable investment opportunities for them. For this to happen there is thus a need for new and financially innovative approaches to be developed by governments in the region that can respond to this interest while also mitigating the stress of rising sovereign indebtedness.[74]

This chapter identifies some of the green finance mechanisms and approaches that can be incorporated by national and local governments, primarily in Southeast Asia, into their post-COVID-19 strategies, but are also useful inputs for domestic commercial banks and private corporates. Each approach would of course need to be designed per the local circumstances but guided by the principles outlined here.

Based on some of the examples seen in the previous chapter, these approaches are split into three types of financial innovation: (i) government catalytic funds, (ii) capital market instruments, and (iii) specific thematic concepts.

A. Government Catalytic Funds

Government funds almost always play the role of de-risking projects from a bankability perspective to catalyze in private, institutional, and commercial funds as seen in the Viability Gap Funds for PPPs in several countries. A proposed concept for green finance facilities for the post-COVID-19 era is outlined here, incorporating concepts from earlier examples.

1. National Green Finance Catalytic Facilities: De-risking Mechanisms

The concept of creating national or local green funds or facilities that can act to de-risk green projects is especially relevant in the post-COVID-19 environment. Risk perceptions over bankability considerations have emerged as a key constraint on private capital flows. As a result, a catalytic facility that can transition green infrastructure projects across the bankability gap and hence attract private finance, is much needed. A structure for a generic green finance facility is provided in Figure 9.

---

[74] N. Robins, A. Pinzon, and M. Hugman. 2020. How Could Sustainable Finance Help Avoid an Emerging Market Sovereign Debt Crunch. *The London School of Economics and Political Science. Grantham Research Institute on Climate Change and the Environment. 26 May.*

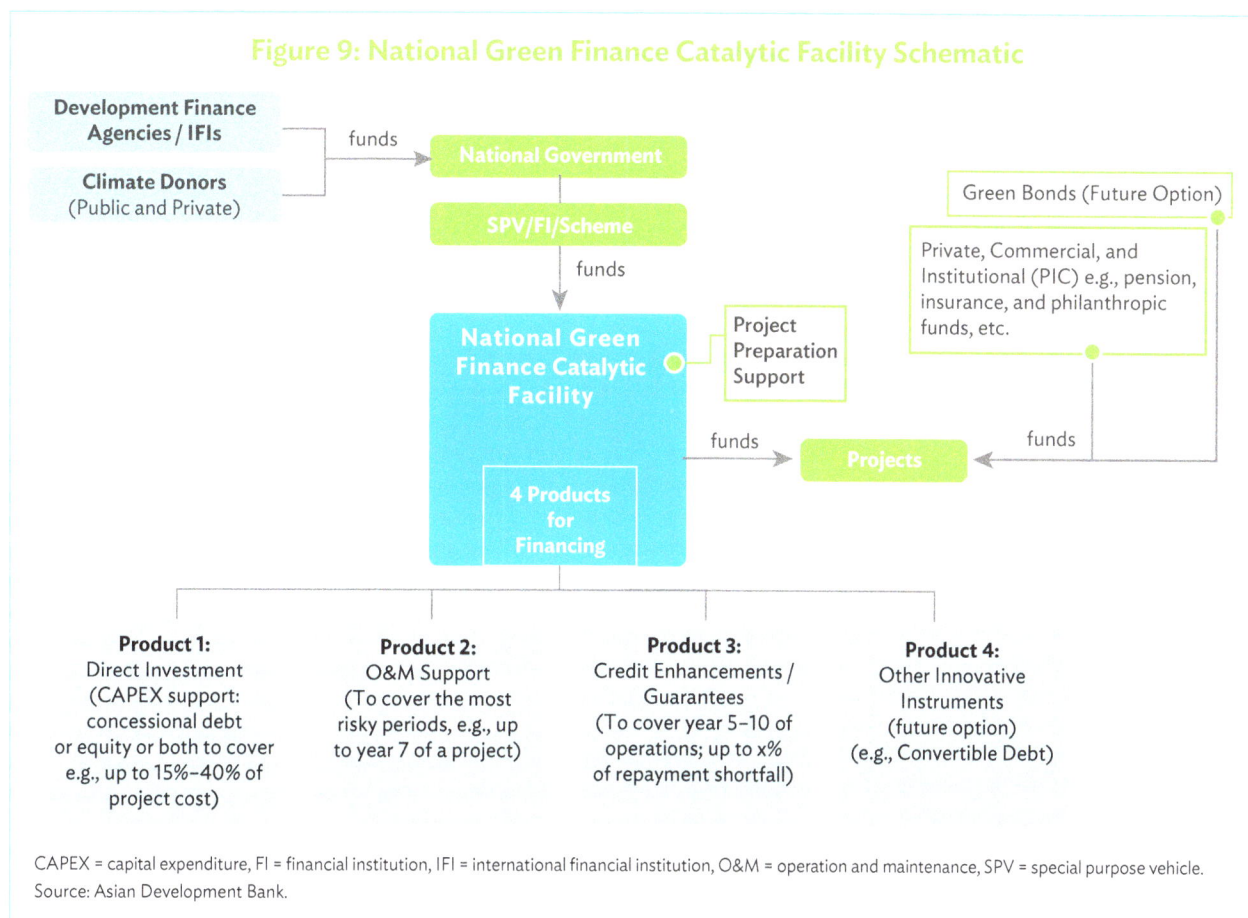

Figure 9: National Green Finance Catalytic Facility Schematic

CAPEX = capital expenditure, FI = financial institution, IFI = international financial institution, O&M = operation and maintenance, SPV = special purpose vehicle.
Source: Asian Development Bank.

Facility versus project. Creating a finance facility in contrast to a stand-alone project approach is beneficial for reasons that include: (i) scale of funds to be attracted; (ii) faster timescales; (iii) efficiency in the administration of a range of funds collated and pooled; and (iv) diversification of risks across a range of sectors and geographies. Such a facility should also combine project structuring and capacity building functions, which is much needed for local government project sponsors and can work to create a pipeline of bankable projects. Cross-learning can also be effectively built up through such a facility, ideally placed at a national government or national development finance institution level. Green frameworks can also be institutionalized at such an entity as well as some of the necessary green policy actions such as project screening mechanisms, reporting, and monitoring, which will give much greater confidence to global investors. A facility that supports projects at various stages of development such as this could also access capital markets through green bonds and raise further capital. Such a programmatic response is critical to rapidly finance post-COVID-19 climate projects and to capitalize on the window of opportunity posed by COVID-19 recovery stimuli.

Incentivizing funds linked to conditionalities. The use of concessional funds from such a facility can be linked to green investment principles at a facility level including certain conditionalities that align with government priorities and will likely include: (i) linkage to clear green impacts; (ii) number and type of green jobs created; (iii) ability to attract a minimum of private capital; and (iv) best leveraging or lowest fiscal impact on government budgets. This last factor could also be the way for governments to compare different projects with those selected that leverage a dollar of government funds in the facility to the maximum level, catalyzing three or more multiples of dollars from the private sector.

Focus and emphasis. Focusing on transformational, high potential climate and green projects, using internationally aligned climate criteria, as well as on bankability and leveraging, through the use of innovative or blended finance approaches, will be vital to crowd in capital from a wide range of sources.

Products offered. The key to the facility will be the actual products it offers to projects and the several forms these can take, just a few of which are noted below. These would need to be aligned with the local context and the sectors that are being prioritized.

- **Grant funds.** The simplest form of de-risking, along the lines of a viability gap fund, could be a product for the most challenging sectors such as for rural development. However, this would create a further fiscal burden on governments and with no possibility of repayment, it does not allow the facility to be sustainable.

- **Revolving transition period capital expenditure loans.** A more sophisticated variant on grants, this is a product that could be well suited for the next 2- to 3-year transition period when the impact of COVID-19 on project revenues might be the hardest. In response, the facility could offer a 3- to 5-year low cost or 0% loan to projects, capped at 15%–40% of project costs. This would considerably reduce the blended capital cost of a project and help in making the project more attractive to private capital.

- **Revenue payments or guarantees or completion guarantees.** A possible product suited to reducing government spending upfront and defraying this to annual payments over a 5- to 10-year period, this could help in bringing in more private capital for capital expenditure. This could also be provided as guarantees and help insulate private capital providers from the uncertainty around revenues.

- **Convertible debt.** A more complex product, this is low-cost debt provided to a project that could be converted into equity once certain financial indicators of a project are achieved. The conversion into equity could also be linked to options for project sponsors or institutional investors to purchase such equity at values that would be attractive for the facility and allow funds to be deployed elsewhere once recouped.

2. Debt for Nature Swap Funds

The concept of debt for nature swaps (DNS) has been around for a long time, with perhaps one of the earliest examples being in 1998 with the United States (US) Tropical Forest Conservation Act (TFCA), which provided debt relief to help protect and sustainably manage tropical forests in beneficiary developing countries. As of December 2014, the program used about $233 million to conclude 20 TFCA debt-for-nature agreements with 14 countries, including Bangladesh, El Salvador, Guatemala, Panama, and the Philippines in return for protection of their forests.[75] The principle of a DNS is fairly simple; an agreement to reduce or cancel the level of debt servicing by a developing country in exchange for a commitment to utilize the resultant saved debt payment for investments in conservation or nature projects. However, its design and impact can be more challenging, requiring both the donor or debt provider and governments to carefully address how the "saved" funds will be used, including consideration of local and indigenous people impacted as well as careful monitoring systems, etc. An example is the Costa Rica DNS supported by the Government of the US along with Conservation International and The Nature Conservancy. In return for a reduction in its debt to the US government, The Nature Conservancy has noted that Costa Rica reversed deforestation with 52% of the country forested again (up from 26%) reversing the past trend of close to an 80% loss of its original forest cover.[76]

The above principle and examples, such as the niche Seychelles Blue Bond, can however be adapted and scaled up for inclusion in green recovery approaches by governments. A hybrid DNS approach is outlined here.

Debt for nature swaps for recovery hybrid approach. Rather than focusing solely on restructuring of existing debts, an option would be to use DNS to attract fresh investment. Governments could create a ring-fenced fund

---

[75] United States Agency for International Development (USAID). Financing Forest Conservation: An Overview of the Tropical Forest and Coral Reef Conservation Act.

[76] NBC News. 2007. Costa Rica gets largest debt-for-nature swap. 17 October.

or vehicle to attract global private sector investors, both debt and equity, into the fund. To reduce both the cost of debt and equity returns expected by investors, even for an initial transition period (perhaps the first 5 to 7 years after the impact of COVID-19) the fund would need a backing guarantee fund or account to provide an assured fixed payment to such investors (in the case of debt investors) or perhaps a guaranteed exit payment to equity investors, for instance, at the end of a 5-year period. For this backing guarantee fund or account to be credible to investors, a portion of government budgets could be set aside or grants and low-cost long tenure debt sought from multilateral development agencies such as the ADB, the Green Climate Fund, the Global Environment Facility, or the World Bank. The impact of this structure would be to reduce the cost of funds raised from private investors and pass on these savings to green projects.

A further design to make the hybrid DNS vehicle above more appealing to investors and hence be willing to accept lower financing rates, would be for the use of funds to be demarcated explicitly for (i) priority or "advanced" green sectors, with low revenue models but greater environmental impacts than standard green projects (methodologies for this exist), such as marine protected areas or agribusiness; and (ii) more commercial green projects, which would allow for some cross subsidizing of returns. Further, instead of funds raised all being provided as upfront funds for project capital expenditures, some portion of the funds could be provided as annual payments to green projects to help them meet their own costs and thus able to leverage in further debt at the project level.

The overall principle in this approach is the reduction of debt payments and hence decreasing the level of indebtedness of a government on the condition that the "savings" are used to channel the funds to explicit green or nature projects, which would thus require careful observation of green frameworks for project selection.

B. Capital Market Instruments

Capital markets are a critical mechanism to access global pools of funds particularly if the markets are highly efficient, well-regulated, liquid, and well performing, thus allowing investors clear exits and transparent procedures to build confidence on.

1.   COVID-19 Recovery Transition Bonds

An approach suggested specifically to build momentum in the capital markets, given the COVID-19 context, is that of the COVID-19 Recovery Transition Bonds (CRTB). These are green bonds tailored and structured to the needs of the time period impacted by COVID-19, supported by government and MDB funds providing risk assurance. They will carry the same level of diligence in terms of green definition to avoid any greenwashing, but with a focus on recovery and an ambition to build back better.

Key features of the instrument, structured as a two-step bond include:

- **Zero coupon period**. The first 5 years of bond repayments to be pegged at a 0% coupon rate. This is designed to enable on-lending of funds raised at concessional rates to projects with very low revenue projections in the next 4–5 years due to COVID-19 impacts.

- **Stepped-up coupon period**. A second period of repayment of between 5 to 15 years (ideally long tenure bonds are better suited for infrastructure), would see bond repayments pegged at a market return, likely on a yield to maturity basis coupon payment. This step-up is suggested to ensure returns to investors who have supported the transition period and enable greater liquidity for the bonds.

The above step-up structure builds on the concept of deep discount bonds that have been undertaken in several instances, including in Asia. For instance, the 10-year Deep Discount Bond (Zero Coupon Bond) of the Rural Electrification Corporation Limited in India, approved for issuance in 2011, also had clear built-in tax provisions (income from such bonds to be taxed as capital gains only on transfer or redemption or maturity).[77] However, there is a risk that zero coupon or deep discount bonds are perceived as inherently risky and are issued at a market price much below face value, more so in circumstances that make COVID-19 impacts unclear. Hence, it will be critical to ensure credit enhancement wraps for these bonds, at least for the initial period. There have been several instances of guarantees or first loss structures being provided in the past to various bonds, including from development agencies, and climate funds such as the Global Environment Facility. Therefore, it is proposed that the CRTB instruments are supported by an assurance fund as detailed below.

The COVID-19 Recovery Transition Bonds Assurance Fund. An assurance fund will be critical to provide credibility to the CRTB structure, with clear guarantee parameters, and hence create an appetite and interest in the global investor community. The fund can be financed from government budgets as well as government-raised sovereign loans from MDBs. Critically, such sovereign funds can also be leveraged to attract funds from private sector investors into the fund. A regional fund can also be created instead of a national fund which can provide guarantees for a group of countries, with a regional example being the ACGF, managed by the ADB. Figure 10 depicts a proposed structure for a CRTB Assurance Fund.

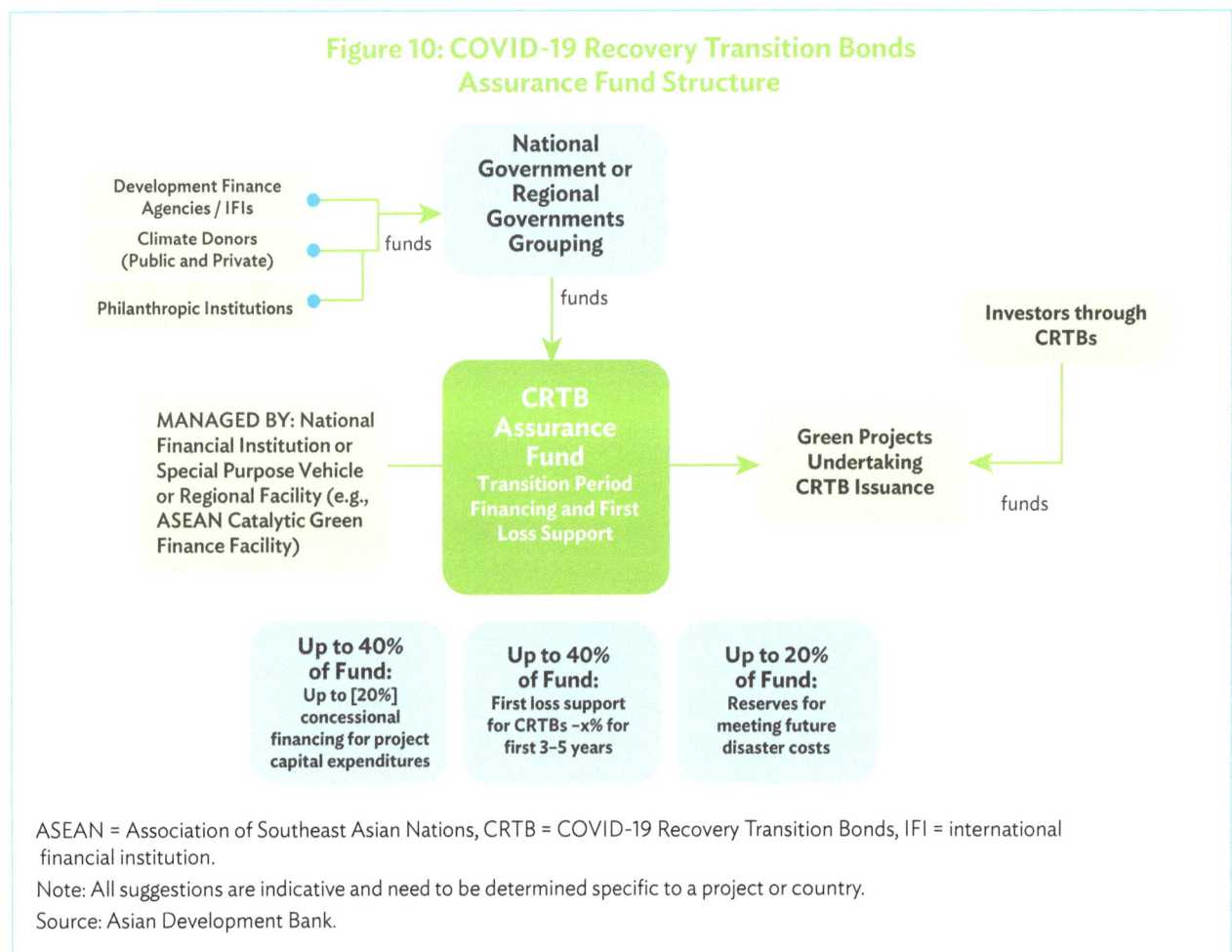

Figure 10: COVID-19 Recovery Transition Bonds Assurance Fund Structure

ASEAN = Association of Southeast Asian Nations, CRTB = COVID-19 Recovery Transition Bonds, IFI = international financial institution.
Note: All suggestions are indicative and need to be determined specific to a project or country.
Source: Asian Development Bank.

Funds usage. The CRTB Assurance Fund would provide guarantees to bonds raised by green projects in the country through a state-owned entity, a PPP entity, or local government entity. Guarantees can be in the form of first loss, exit guarantees, and completion guarantees. A guaranteed exit payment offered to investors at a specific

---

[77] A. Rey. 2010. REC Seeks RBI Approval to Sell Zero-Coupon Bonds to Bank. *Economic Times*. 18 November.

time, perhaps 6 years after the initial investment (assuming 3–4 years for construction completion and at least 1–2 years of operations), could create the appropriate incentives for investors.

In addition to guarantees to CRTBs, the fund could also provide some concessional financing (either as debt or convertible grant or debt) to green projects, especially if these are seen as riskier projects due to greater revenue risks (e.g., social sector projects) or construction difficulties (e.g., extensive tunneling). This blends the concept of a viability gap fund with bond guarantees and might be more attractive for investors showing interest in the fund. Any provision of such financing should be linked not only to green eligibility but also financial bankability thresholds, such that support is only provided up to the level of need (for instance, the debt service coverage ratio exceeds a minimum level of 1.05) to attract private capital.

A portion of funds could also be invested in liquid assets such as government securities to be available to governments to meet quick response financing in the case of future disasters. This combination of uses for the fund should provide both an assurance to investors while also allowing it to be financially sustainable and thereby protecting government liabilities.

2. Sustainable Impact Bonds

COVID-19 bonds could also be issued to be aligned with social or sustainability impact funds. Issued by state-owned enterprises, local governments, or sovereigns. These would aim to finance only projects that have a positive impact on the climate (based on a recognized green framework or taxonomy such as that of the ACGF or Climate Bonds Initiative) and on a sector impacted by the pandemic. This directly links the use of proceeds with green, social, or sustainability impacts especially relevant for COVID-19 responses.

Thematic areas. Priorities that would define the use of funds could include oceans and river health, air quality, biodiversity and wildlife conservation, climate change, livelihood protection, sustainable tourism, waste management, and natural produce management. Defining such themes will be important to target the appropriate investor base.

Impact linked incentives. Similar to social impact loans, the structure of such bonds could include financial incentives to meet or exceed targets. Such targets could, for instance, include green job creation, carbon dioxide emissions reduction, and implementation timelines. The achievement of such targets could lead to better financing terms, such as lower interest rates or extension of loan tenures, at the project level, which could also be reflected in reduced coupon payments to bond holders. Conversely, the bond would need to pay more to bondholders if predetermined ESG targets are not achieved, creating an incentive for the ESG targets to be met.

The primary difference between ESG-linked debt and traditional green debt is that ESG-linked debt can be spent on anything as long as the targets are achieved in an agreed timeframe, whereas traditional green debt has strict guidelines about what can be done with the proceeds. Another important distinction is that these instruments may be available to a wider range of sectors and companies that would not normally qualify for green bonds, but they can still make a significant positive contribution to sustainability.

Transition bonds. Governments could also look to helping companies in the "brown" sectors in the region develop transition bonds to go greener. Sectors such as meat farming and heavy industry, while employing significant numbers of people, urgently need to reduce their GHG emissions and need capital to achieve such efforts. Such transition bonds, sometimes seen as controversial, would need very clear and transparent monitoring systems and clear targets to be achieved that could provide a way for such companies to access the global investor base. Governments and multilateral agencies would need to help develop the appropriate standards and monitoring systems to ensure that funds raised meet the required green criteria.

3. Green Securitization

An instrument of growing interest is that of green securitization. Securitization is a well-established practice in global debt capital markets. It is the process of converting assets into securities, which are then financed through the capital markets via the issuance of an asset backed security (ABS) bond or note. What differentiates it from traditional bonds is that an ABS is collateralized or secured by classes of assets and typically an income stream from those assets, thereby reducing the risk to the bond holder. Credit enhancements in the form of over-collateralization, guarantees, liquidity facilities, first loss pieces, and cofinancing strengthen the structure. Securitization can be equally applicable for refinancing green, blue, or any other environment-related assets. Securitization is a fast-developing and recent part of this market. The Association for Financial Markets in Europe (AFME) published a position paper, highlighting the growing interest in this area from the investor community.[78]

Green securitization consists of the following types:

(i) **Capital relief securitization.** Bond proceeds are used to purchase assets from a project sponsor, thereby relieving sponsor capital to be further invested in the green space, for instance from a bank that can then use the new capital to give green loans.

(ii) **Green asset collateral.** Bond proceeds used to purchase existing assets from green projects, such as typically seen in green bonds.

(iii) **Green bond securitization.** Like a collateralized debt obligation (CDO), a pool of green bonds could be sold into a securitization structure for refinancing.

(iv) **Use of proceeds.** Bond proceeds are used to invest in new green projects.

Green securitization for post-COVID-19 recovery. Green securitization can be a tool for providing the large liquidity needed from a wider global investor base, in developing country industries impacted by losses from the COVID-19 pandemic. Effectively these can be structured as typical asset finance securitizations using projected cash flows and a green element, with flexibility in the terms and conditions needed to help on the road to recovery, e.g., longer grace periods, tradable market instruments, and ratings. Potentially such an approach could lower funding costs relative to unsecured green bonds due to the availability of collateral, with the appeal further improved by guarantees from governments and MDBs. A form of such securitization is illustrated below.

Future flow securitization. Under these types of structures, the originator is able to monetize the value of expected *future* cash flows from revenue or sales (Figure 11). Typical sectors that could be helped would be those affected severely by the pandemic. The transportation industry, exports with trade receivables, the auto industry, public utilities, and toll roads, where regular income streams have been disrupted, would be prime candidates. The assumption is that following a certain transition period, these cash flows would return and allow the sectors to become self-sustaining again. As the lending would be done under capital market regulation, governance, accountability, performance-linked fund deployment, and standard market practices would all ensure a more efficient use of finances and better leveraging of government and multilateral support. Further, the structure would allow for green principles, processes, and methods to be an integral part of the lending decision.

The securitization could be in local, regional or global capital markets, depending on several factors, including the currency denomination of the assets, the ability of hedging instruments, and the investor demand.

---

[78] AFME. 2019. Principles for Developing a Green Securitisation Market in Europe—Position Paper.

Figure 11: Future Flow Securitization

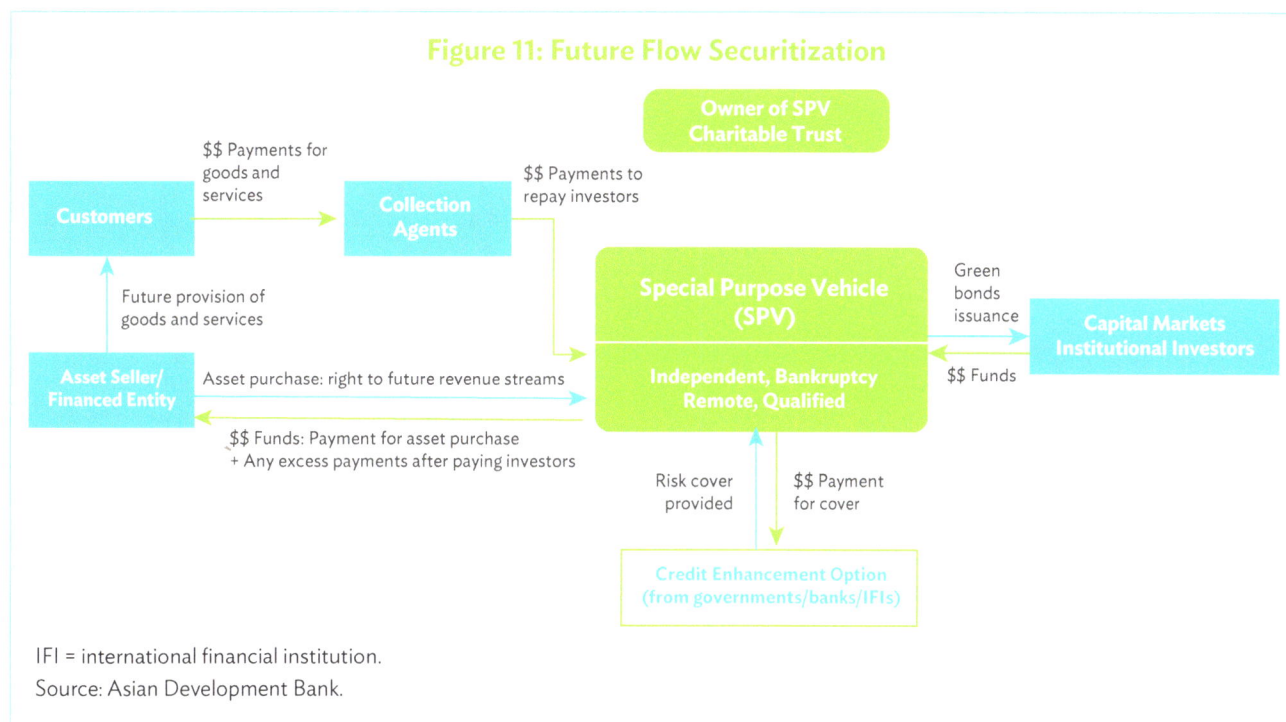

IFI = international financial institution.
Source: Asian Development Bank.

Box 4: Future Flow Securitization for the Airline Industry—An Illustration

Taking the example of the airline industry, affected by losses from flight disruptions and loss of ticket sales, while its high costs—lease payments for aircrafts, buildings and infrastructure, and operational costs—continue, would require

- short-term emergency funding to repay immediate operational costs to avoid defaulting and thus bankruptcy and
- long-term bridge financing until it can operate normally and generate enough revenues to refinance itself.

Assuming the airline can expect revenues from ticket sales, and sub-leasing its services to other smaller airlines, plus indirect revenues from onboard sales of goods, it could raise funds on the back of its anticipated future earnings. These could be denominated in dollars and local currency.

A special purpose vehicle (SPV) would need to be established for the transaction, with the airline company selling a portion of its revenues to the SPV under a revenue sharing sale agreement. This asset would be bought from proceeds of a bond issuance to capital market securitization investors backed by its right to receive the existing and future airline revenues.

Under the terms of the bond, there would be a grace period equal to the transition period for payment of principal and coupon, thereby allowing the airline time to recover. Green criteria such as reducing the airlines carbon footprint on the ground and in the air through fewer short haul flights, reduced long haul flights, use of greener fuel, and green infrastructure policies, would be a prerequisite for inclusion in the structure.

At the end of the transition period, scheduled payments of interest and principal will be paid from the revenue streams until the maturity of the bond. With a positive track record, the airline would have the potential to repay the bond investors by: (i) reissuing the bonds at more favorable coupons and potentially less support from a government, (ii) issuing a corporate bond, and (iii) borrowing from commercial sources.

This would lead to a more sustainable financing model and a favorable blended financing methodology where different financing sources are used as risk changes. Importantly, any financing from the government and the Asian Development Bank would have the potential to revert to them as well. There is also an upside for the airline in case they perform better than expected; they would retain any additional revenues.

Source: Asian Development Bank.

C. Specific Thematic Concepts

Governments could also develop specific approaches for certain sectors recognized as requiring more focus, either for responding to this pandemic or future potential epidemics. Such approaches could also envelop the creation of opportunities for a country whether in job creation or establishing an industry's competitive advantage in the region for longer-term economic growth. Two key sectors in this regard are health care and water pollution, which represent both a challenge and an opportunity for countries to focus attention on. Some suggested proposals are presented in this section.

1. Integrated Health and Sustainable Infrastructure Clusters

This concept of sustainable infrastructure clusters builds on both the economic zones idea and the need for long-term health-care sector improvements.

Integrated components. The proposal (Figure 12) aims to develop a cluster or zone of high-quality research and development (R&D) medical facilities, along with specialist hospitals and vaccine manufacturing, thus integrating the health-care value chain. While these facilities are to be developed through PPPs, the government would need to fund infrastructure for the cluster as well as provide low-cost loans for facilities with higher risk probabilities, mainly the R&D facilities. A zone or cluster might be a new build outside urban areas or rehabilitation of existing areas within a city. The intention would be to ensure these are all built as green constructions with access to renewable energy and incorporating energy efficiency and natural resource conservation measures.

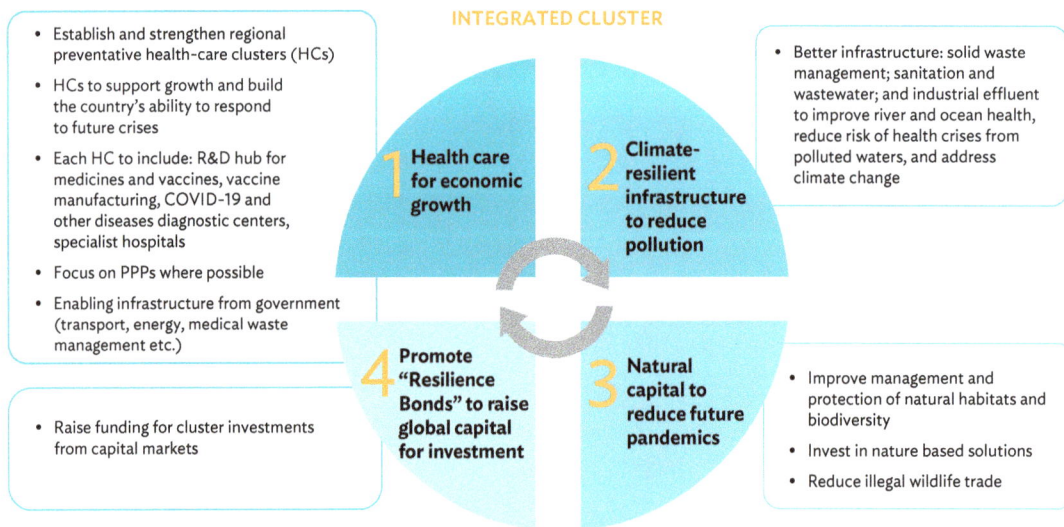

Figure 12: Health Care for Well-Being and Infrastructure Clusters

INTEGRATED CLUSTER

- Establish and strengthen regional preventative health-care clusters (HCs)
- HCs to support growth and build the country's ability to respond to future crises
- Each HC to include: R&D hub for medicines and vaccines, vaccine manufacturing, COVID-19 and other diseases diagnostic centers, specialist hospitals
- Focus on PPPs where possible
- Enabling infrastructure from government (transport, energy, medical waste management etc.)

- Raise funding for cluster investments from capital markets

1 Health care for economic growth

2 Climate-resilient infrastructure to reduce pollution

4 Promote "Resilience Bonds" to raise global capital for investment

3 Natural capital to reduce future pandemics

- Better infrastructure: solid waste management; sanitation and wastewater; and industrial effluent to improve river and ocean health, reduce risk of health crises from polluted waters, and address climate change

- Improve management and protection of natural habitats and biodiversity
- Invest in nature based solutions
- Reduce illegal wildlife trade

COVID-19 = coronavirus disease, PPP = public-private partnership, R&D = research and development.
Source: Asian Development Bank.

Along with health-care components, a cluster should also link to the development of associated water or ocean pollution infrastructure as well as low carbon or clean infrastructure to reduce air pollution (clean energy, clean transport, and air quality management) within the cluster or in close proximity. This is with the aim of integrating both prevention components, from reducing pollution in water bodies for instance, with curative components such as hospitals.

Integrated for easier fund raising. The cluster approach is also important in that it allows the blending of better revenue-generating components with lower revenue-generating and riskier components in the value chain, providing a more attractive combined proposition to private sector entities.

Resilience bonds. The concept also includes a financing program through bonds to be undertaken by national or local governments to raise funds for such clusters. Such bond programs, likely with a measure of credit enhancement from governments, should be able to leverage government budgets to raise funds from private capital investors and funds.

Other combinations. While Figure 12 uses a cluster-based approach, the proposed areas are not meant to be prescriptive but could be used as a template approach customized to the context. For example, significant work has been done on sustainable urban development that integrates policy aims (to foster trade and investment and community linkages), regional connectivity, and sustainable impacts (smart cities) by the ASEAN Secretariat 2018, ASEAN Sustainable Urbanisation Strategy (ASUS) and the ASEAN Smart Cities Network (ASCN), under the Master Plan on ASEAN Connectivity 2025.[79] The ASUS provides a possible cluster approach for urban development that could also fit this concept, suggesting a framework of sustainable urbanization around six areas and 18 sub-areas (Figure 13).

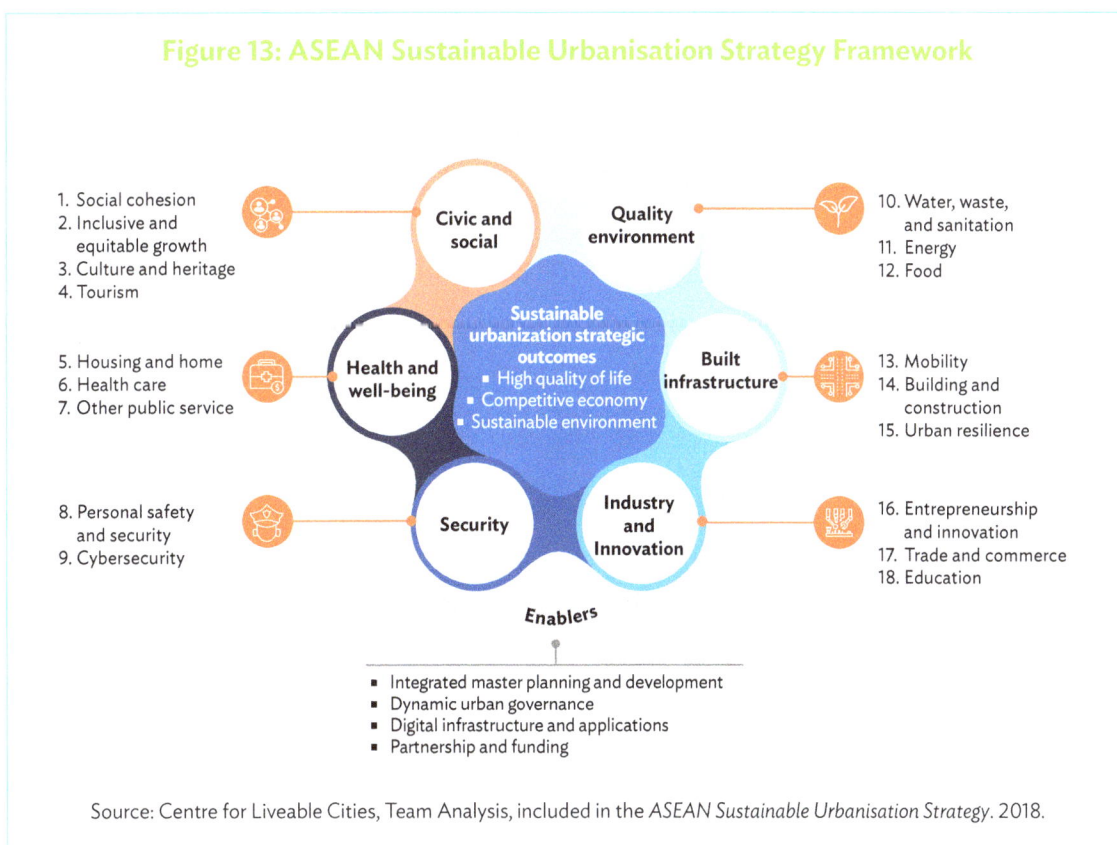

Figure 13: ASEAN Sustainable Urbanisation Strategy Framework

Source: Centre for Liveable Cities, Team Analysis, included in the *ASEAN Sustainable Urbanisation Strategy*. 2018.

---

[79] ASEAN. 2018. ASEAN Sustainable Urbanisation Strategy.

2. Oceans Financing and Blue Credits

Pandemics and oceans health. An increasing body of work links climate change, biodiversity loss, and ocean acidification with human health. Pandemics such as COVID-19 seem to be a result of blurring the lines between human livelihoods and the natural environment. A 2012 report noted the emergence of approximately one virus a year from an animal host due to changes in local ecosystems disturbing the balance between pathogens and principal host species, together with increasing urbanization and changes in human behavior.[80]

The oceans, a term used to denote all water bodies, whether seas, lakes, or rivers, are critical as they absorb, together with the forests, around 50% of global carbon dioxide emissions. Rising ocean pollution is reducing their ability to act as carbon sinks, propelling us further toward global warming over the 2 degrees level. With ever warmer ocean currents and the melting of glaciers, there is expected to be an increase in viruses and future pandemics.

Further, with the massive rise in seawater acidity, estimated at 30% since the industrial revolution combined with pollutants such as 8 million tons of plastics ending up in the oceans each year, the threat to the many fishing communities and economies that depend on the oceans cannot be overstated. The oceans economy is equivalent to the seventh largest economy in the world measured by contribution to gross domestic product, with the value of goods and services from coastal and marine environments estimated at about $2.5 trillion a year, extraction of marine resources worth $6.9 trillion, and tourism and coastline industries amounting to $7.8 trillion.[81]

The need for governments to specifically focus on reducing pollution and other negative impacts on their water resources is thus urgent. Caring for the oceans should be included in economic recovery strategies. Innovative financing approaches can help in this to scale up the financing available for oceans health projects.

Blue finance challenges. Therefore, there is a need for "blue finance" or "blue capital" to support ocean health projects whether in urban, coastal, or rural areas. Blue finance has gained interest from both conservationists and investors, underlining the connection between ocean protection and finance, given the growing awareness of their economic value (footnote 81).

However, a lack of blue economy projects has been the major constraint, not a lack of capital or investor interest. A survey by Credit Suisse and Responsible Investor covering 328 respondents from 34 countries, analyzed factors such as interest, barriers, and opportunities in the blue economy and listed the lack of investment grade projects, internal expertise, and visibility as key barriers to mainstreaming blue finance (Figure 14).[82]

In developing Asia especially, many blue economy projects are constrained by low tariff and revenue levels due to affordability considerations, or are pure cost projects with no revenue streams at all. Other risk factors from high cost technology needs in sectors such as plastic waste management, the environment and land acquisition have deterred private capital sources from these sectors leading to a growing demand–supply gap in needed infrastructure.

The blue credits mechanism. One mechanism that could be developed by countries in their green recovery strategies post-COVID-19, is to create a mechanism of "blue credits," to specifically address the issue of a lack of low revenue streams so as to catalyze commercial capital.

Based on several existing concepts such as the annuity model in the roads PPP sector, the model would essentially entail a local or national government providing a predetermined annual payment to a blue economy project

---

[80]   C. R. Howard and N. F. Fletcher. 2012. Emerging Virus Diseases: Can We Ever Expect the Unexpected? *Emerg Microbes Infect.* 1 (12). pp. 1–9. 26 December.

[81]   H. Avery. 2018. It's Time for Blue Finance. *Euromoney.* 5 June.

[82]   Responsible Investor and Credit Suisse. 2020. *Investors and the Blue Economy. Ocean Risk or Opportunity? Is the Blue Economy Investible?*

Figure 14: Investor Opportunities in the Sustainable Blue Economy

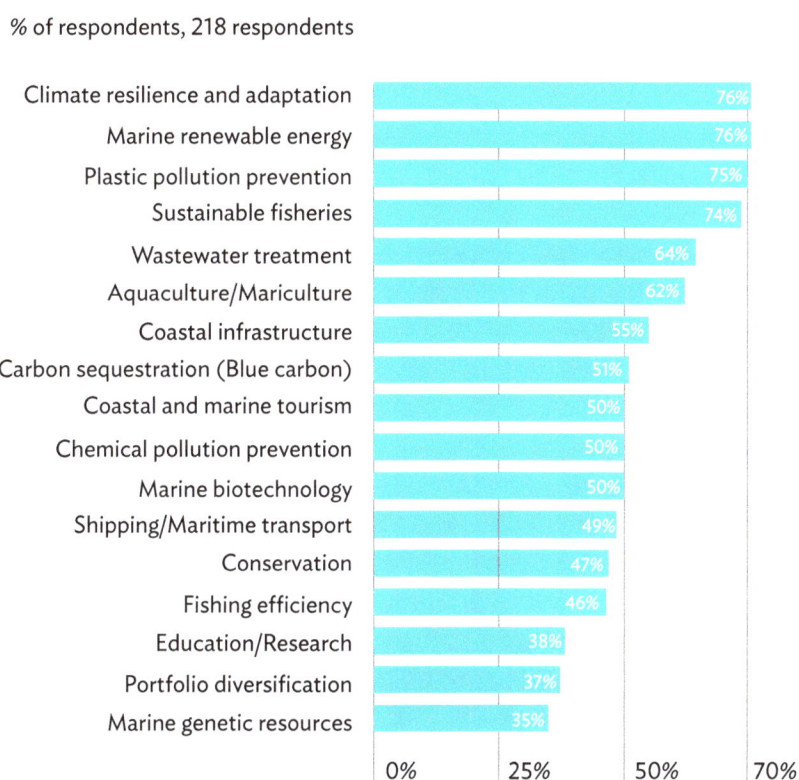

% of respondents, 218 respondents

Category	%
Climate resilience and adaptation	76%
Marine renewable energy	76%
Plastic pollution prevention	75%
Sustainable fisheries	74%
Wastewater treatment	64%
Aquaculture/Mariculture	62%
Coastal infrastructure	55%
Carbon sequestration (Blue carbon)	51%
Coastal and marine tourism	50%
Chemical pollution prevention	50%
Marine biotechnology	50%
Shipping/Maritime transport	49%
Conservation	47%
Fishing efficiency	46%
Education/Research	38%
Portfolio diversification	37%
Marine genetic resources	35%

Source: Responsible Investor and Credit Suisse. 2020.

(whether implemented by a state-owned enterprise or a PPP). Using predetermined indicators, such as chemical oxygen demand and biochemical oxygen demand levels that the project needs to show at set points in time, payment streams or credits would kick in when these events are triggered.

Some funding support as low-cost "blue credit" loans could also be provided for capital expenditure under the mechanism, but the main aim would be for the private sector to finance most of the capital expenditure and then focus on implementation efficiencies with insulation from revenue risks. The added value enhancing calculation to be included here would be for the blue credit payments to be capped at the projected costs to governments from *not* undertaking such projects, for instance health costs from diseases arising from polluted river bodies or decline in fishing stocks in a local area.

These relatively easy measures would enhance the rationale for why such credits are necessary. The payment mechanism for such blue credits could be ring-fenced into dedicated special purpose vehicles, which could be the recipient of funds from MDBs and private sector entities that would also perhaps issue blue bonds in time.

Creating a visible mechanism such as this would signal a government's intent clearly and strongly to both project sponsors and private capital sources. It would also create clear momentum for leveraging private capital amounting to three or four times the amount of government funds into projects.

Including such mechanisms, along with credible sovereign funds into post-COVID-19 recovery packages would be a critical step forward in refocusing attention on this hugely critical theme and lead to safer, healthier, and sustainable economic growth in the region.

5 SEEKING SUPPORT FROM ADB AND THE ASEAN CATALYTIC GREEN FINANCE FACILITY

People wearing protective face mask in Jakarta, Indonesia on 27 March 2020. (photo by Afriadi Hikmal/ADB)

This paper has been developed with support from the ACGF, administered by the ADB on behalf of the ASEAN member states. The ACGF and ADB can provide support to countries in developing green recovery strategies. Both can also assist with working through some of the above concepts specifically from among a number of support tools listed here, subject to due processes and government and respective board approvals.

- **ADB technical assistance.** Normally in the form of grants, this can support developing member countries in knowledge and capacity development, policy inputs, and project preparation. This support can be used to design some of the fund or bond structures noted in the previous chapter.

- **ACGF technical assistance.** The ACGF includes a tool for Rapid Assessment Studies for several activities which is supporting the development of new facilities such as the SDG Indonesia One - Green Finance Facility, and social and sustainability bonds in the region. The ACGF is also supporting a green investment opportunities report in the Philippines, with the Climate Bonds Initiative, to identify a long list of projects.

- **Loan funds.** Loan funds from ADB's sovereign window can be augmented by the ACGF's two-step loan (sovereign guaranteed) designed to catalyze private capital through a de-risking pricing approach.

- **Guarantee.** These products are also available through ADB.

6 CONCLUSION

Myagdi river along the Beni–Darbang road.
(photo by Samir Jung Thapa/ADB).

The purpose of this paper has been to highlight innovative finance concepts and examples that might help governments plan their post-COVID-19 economic recovery strategies so as to build back better, with green, sustainable, and inclusive priorities.

Global thinkers are increasingly acknowledging the critical role of green infrastructure in supporting economic growth and livelihoods, while also ensuring the sustainability of the planet's extremely critical balance of natural resources and achieving the Paris Agreement targets of a less than 2-degree rise in temperatures. The IMF Managing Director Kristalina Georgieva, calling for recovery efforts to catalyze a green transition, has noted that "a 'green recovery' is our bridge to a more resilient future."[83] Private capital investors have echoed the same, such as the Institutional Investor Group on Climate Change, which collectively manages nearly half of all global capital investments worth over $34 trillion. The group cautioned that "As governments pursue efforts to recover from this economic downturn, they should not lose sight of the climate crisis." It emphasized that "Governments should avoid the prioritization of risky, short-term emissions-intensive projects."[84]

Such green strategies and infrastructure investments provide a limited window of opportunity to push for investments that significantly reduce greenhouse gas emissions, reduce energy intensity, and support the restoration of carbon sinks. Investing in green infrastructure will stimulate economic recovery and create much-needed jobs.

DBS and the United Nations Environment Inquiry estimate that the size of the green finance opportunity in ASEAN (before COVID-19) was $3 trillion from 2016 to 2030. This encompasses four sectors: infrastructure, renewable energy and energy efficiency, food and agriculture, and land use.[85] Building the green economy through infrastructure in Southeast Asia will create local employment through managing and operating sustainable transport systems, managing green buildings and energy distribution systems, and operating sustainable agriculture supply chains.

Governments will need to use innovative financing mechanisms and approaches to attract much needed private capital for such green infrastructure investments, especially now that project risk perceptions will be higher. The leveraging and de-risking role of governments in catalyzing the needed finance, including accelerating the momentum of green capital markets, will be critical.

ADB, through its long-established presence in the region, can provide the support needed whether finance, policy, capacity building, or the development of green mechanisms.

[83]   A. Shalal. 2020. IMF Leader Says Pandemic Stimulus Must Focus on Battling Climate Crisis. *Reuters*. 29 April.

[84]   F. Simon. 2020. Financiers Join EU 'Green Recovery Alliance'. *Euractive.com*. 5 May.

[85]   United Nations Environment Programme and DBS. 2017. Green Finance Opportunities in ASEAN.

Bibliography

ABS-CBN News. 2020. "Build Build Build" a Priority as Philippines Resets from Pandemic: NEDA Chief. 30 April. https://news.abs-cbn.com/business/04/30/20/build-build-build-a-priority-as-philippines-resets-from-pandemic-neda-chief.

Akhlas, A. W. 2020. $3.9 billion State Spending Reallocated for COVID-19 Response: Sri Mulyani. *Jakarta Post.* https://www.thejakartapost.com/news/2020/03/20/3-9-billion-state-spending-reallocated-for-covid-19-response-sri-mulyani.html.

Asian Development Bank (ADB). 2009. *The Economics of Climate Change in Southeast Asia.* Manila. https://www.adb.org/publications/economics-climate-change-southeast-asia-regional-review.

———. 2016. *Southeast Asia and the Economics of Global Climate Stabilization.* Manila. January. https://www.adb.org/publications/southeast-asia-economics-global-climate-stabilization.

———. 2017. *Meeting Asia's Infrastructure Needs.* Manila. February. https://www.adb.org/sites/default/files/publication/227496/special-report-infrastructure.pdf.

———. 2018. *Strategy 2030. Achieving a Prosperous, Inclusive, Resilient, and Sustainable Asia and the Pacific.* Manila. July. https://www.adb.org/sites/default/files/institutional-document/435391/strategy-2030-main-document.pdf.

———. 2019. *Action Plan for Healthy Oceans and Sustainable Blue Economies.* Manila. May. https://www.adb.org/sites/default/files/am-content/484066/action-plan-flyer-20190430.pdf.

———. 2020. *Asian Development Outlook (ADO) 2020: What Drives Innovation in Asia?* April. https://www.adb.org/publications/asian-development-outlook-2020-innovation-asia.

———. 2020. An Updated Assessment of the Economic Impact of COVID-19. *ADB Brief* No.133. Manila. May. https://www.adb.org/publications/updated-assessment-economic-impact-covid-19.

———. 2020. *Asian Development Outlook 2020 Supplement: Lockdown, Loosening, and Asia's Growth Prospects.* Manila. June. https://www.adb.org/publications/ado-supplement-june-2020.

———. 2020. Catalyzing Climate Finance with the Shandong Green Development Fund. *ADB Briefs* No. 144. July. https://www.adb.org/sites/default/files/publication/615076/climate-finance-shandong-green-development-fund.pdf.

———. 2020. COVID-19, Technology, and Polarizing Jobs. *ADB Briefs* No. 147. August. https://www.adb.org/sites/default/files/publication/623036/covid-19-technology-polarizing-jobs.pdf.

Asian Development Bank (ADB) and International Labour Organization (ILO). 2020. *Tackling the COVID-19 Youth Employment Crisis in Asia and the Pacific.* https://www.adb.org/sites/default/files/publication/626046/covid-19-youth-employment-crisis-asia-pacific.pdf.

Association for Financial Markets in Europe (AFME). 2019. *Principles for Developing a Green Securitisation Market in Europe—Position Paper.* https://www.afme.eu/Portals/0/globalassets/downloads/briefing-notes/2017/110919%20AFME%20Green%20Securitisation%20Position%20Paper.pdf?ver=2019-09-11-144252-467.

Association of Southeast Asian Nations (ASEAN) Secretariat. 2016. *Master Plan on ASEAN Connectivity.* https://asean.org/storage/2016/09/Master-Plan-on-ASEAN-Connectivity-20251.pdf.

———. 2018. *ASEAN Sustainable Urbanisation Strategy.* https://asean.org/?static_post=asean-sustainable-urbanisation-strategy.

ASEAN Briefing. 2020. Indonesia Launches National Economic Recovery Program. https://www.aseanbriefing.com/news/indonesia-launches-national-economic-recovery-program/.

———. 2020. Malaysia Issues Stimulus Package to Combat COVID-19 Impact. https://www.aseanbriefing.com/news/malaysia-issues-stimulus-package-combat-covid-19-impact/.

ASEAN Capital Markets Forum. Initiatives. Sustainable Finance. Development of a Sustainable Asset Class in ASEAN. https://www.theacmf.org/initiatives/sustainable-finance/development-of-a-sustainable-asset-class-in-asean.

ASEAN Catalytic Green Finance Facility (ACGF). 2020. *Investment Principles and Eligibility Criteria.* April. https://www.adb.org/sites/default/files/institutional-document/601241/acgf-investment-principles-eligibility-criteria.pdf.

Avery, H. 2018. It's Time for Blue Finance. *Euromoney.* 5 June. https://www.euromoney.com/article/b18frlsbst629t/it39s-time-for-blue-finance?copyrightInfo=true.

Belmiloud, S. 2019. Marfrig's Transition Bond: A Low-Carbon Transition or More of the Same. *The FAIRR Initiative.* 22 August. https://www.fairr.org/article/marfrigs-transition-bond/.

Borrell, J. 2020. "Team Europe"—Global EU Response to Covid-19 Supporting Partner Countries and Fragile Populations. *European External Action Service.* 11 April. https://eeas.europa.eu/headquarters/headquarters-homepage_en/77470/%E2%80%9CTeam%20Europe%E2%80%9D%20-%20Global%20EU%20Response%20to%20Covid-19%20supporting%20partner%20countries%20and%20fragile%20populations.

Caraballo, M. U. 2020. SBWS Payout Hits P44B. *The Manila Times.* 15 June. https://www.manilatimes.net/2020/06/15/business/business-top/sbws-payout-hits-p44b/731786/.

Climate Bonds Initiative (CBI). 2019. *Climate Bonds Standard Version 3.0.* December. https://www.climatebonds.net/files/files/climate-bonds-standard-v3-20191210.pdf.

———. 2020. *The ASEAN Green Finance State of the Market* 2019. https://www.climatebonds.net/files/reports/cbi_asean_sotm_2019_final.pdf.

———. 2020. Climate Bonds Initiative Market Summary H1 2020. August. https://www.climatebonds.net/resources/reports/green-bonds-market-summary-h1-2020.

Climate & Development Knowledge Network. 2013. Vietnam's National Green Growth Strategy. April. https://cdkn.org/2013/04/feature-vietnams-national-green-growth-strategy/?loclang=en_gb.

The Coalition of Finance Ministers for Climate Action. 2020. *Better Recovery, Better World: Resetting Climate Action in the Aftermath of the COVID-19 Pandemic.* July. https://www.financeministersforclimate.org/news/better-recovery-better-world-resetting-climate-action-aftermath-covid-19-pandemic.

The Coalition of Finance Ministers for Climate Action. Helsinki Principles. https://www.financeministersforclimate.org/node/273.

Convergence. 2019. Case Study: Climate Finance Facility. *Green Bank Network.* June. https://greenbanknetwork.org/wp-content/uploads/2019/07/Convergence__Climate_Finance_Facility_Case_Study__2019.pdf.

Cooney, M., M. Goldstein, and E. Shapiro. 2019. How Marine Protected Areas Help Fisheries and Ocean Ecosystems. *Centre for American Progress.* https://www.americanprogress.org/issues/green/reports/2019/06/03/470585/marine-protected-areas-help-fisheries-ocean-ecosystems/.

De Vera, B. O. 2020. Economic Team Slash 2020 Infra Budget. *Inquirer.Net.* 19 May. https://business.inquirer.net/297672/economic-team-slashes-2020-infra-budget.

Eckstein, D. et al. 2020. Global Climate Risk Index 2020: Who Suffers Most from Extreme Weather Events? *Germanwatch Briefing Paper.* https://germanwatch.org/sites/germanwatch.org/files/20-2-01e%20Global%20Climate%20Risk%20Index%202020_14.pdf.

Engel, H. et al. 2020. How a Post-Pandemic Stimulus Can Both Create Jobs and Help the Climate. McKinsey & Company. 27 May. https://www.mckinsey.com/business-functions/sustainability/our-insights/how-a-post-pandemic-stimulus-can-both-create-jobs-and-help-the-climate.

Environmental Finance. 2017. Project Bond of the Year—AP Renewables. 7 April. https://www.environmental-finance.com/content/awards/green-bond-awards-2017/winners/project-bond-of-the-year-ap-renewables.html.

European Commission. 2019. Communication from the European Commission to the European Parliament, the European Council, the Council, the European Economic and Social Committee and the Committee of the Regions. The European Green Deal. Brussels. 11 December. https://ec.europa.eu/info/sites/info/files/european-green-deal-communication_en.pdf. https://ec.europa.eu/info/publications/communication-european-green-deal_en.

————. 2020. The European Green Deal Investment Plan and Just Transition Mechanism explained. 14 January. https://ec.europa.eu/commission/presscorner/detail/en/qanda_20_24.

————. 2020. Frans Timmermans' opening remarks at the Petersberg Climate Dialogue. 28 April. https://ec.europa.eu/clima/news/frans-timmermans-opening-remarks-petersberg-climate-dialogue_en.

————. 2020. Sustainable Finance: Commission welcomes the adoption by the European Parliament of the Taxonomy Regulation. 18 June. https://ec.europa.eu/commission/presscorner/detail/en/ip_20_1112.

European Council. 2020. A Recovery Plan for Europe. July. https://www.consilium.europa.eu/en/policies/eu-recovery-plan/.

Farand, C. 2020. South Korea to Implement Green New Deal after Ruling Party Election Win. *Climate Home News.* 16 April. https://www.climatechangenews.com/2020/04/16/south-korea-implement-green-new-deal-ruling-party-election-win/.

Finance in Common. https://financeincommon.org.

Financial Times. 2020. The "Transition" Bonds Bridging the Gap Between Green and Brown. 3 January. https://www.ft.com/content/ff2b3e88-21b0-11ea-92da-f0c92e957a96.

Food and Agriculture Organization of the United Nations. 2013. *Tackling Climate Change Through Livestock: A Global Assessment of Emissions and Mitigation Opportunities.* Rome. http://www.fao.org/3/a-i3437e.pdf.

Garrett-Peltier, H. 2017. Green versus brown: Comparing the employment impacts of energy efficiency, renewable energy, and fossil fuels using an input-output model. Economic Modelling, Elsevier. 61(C). pp. 439-447. https://ideas.repec.org/a/eee/ecmode/v61y2017icp439-447.html.

Global Commission on Adaptation. 2019. Global Leaders Call for Urgent Action on Climate Adaptation; Commission Finds Adaptation Can Deliver $7.1 Trillion in Benefits. 10 September. https://gca.org/global-commission-on-adaptation/commission-news/global-leaders-call-for-urgent-action-on-climate-adaptation-commission-finds-adaptation-can-deliver-7-1-trillion-in-benefits.

The Global Commission on the Economy and Climate. 2018. *Unlocking the Inclusive Growth Story of the 21st Century: Accelerating Climate Action in Urgent Times.* Key Findings and Executive Summary. https://newclimateeconomy. report/2018/wp-content/uploads/sites/6/2018/09/NCE_2018Report_ExecutiveSummary.pdf.

Global Fishing Watch. https://globalfishingwatch.org/.

Global Sustainable Investment Alliance. 2018. *2018 Global Sustainable Investment Review.* http://www.gsi-alliance. org/trends-report-2018/.

———. 2019. *Sustainable Investor Poll on TCFD Implementation.* December. http://www.gsi-alliance.org/members-resources/sustainable-investor-poll-on-tcfd-implementation/.

Government of Cambodia, National Council on Green Growth. 2013. *National Strategic Plan on Green Growth 2013–2030.* https://www.greengrowthknowledge.org/national-documents/cambodia-national-strategic-plan-green-growth-2013-2030.

Government of Indonesia, PT Sarana Multi Infrastruktur. 2020. SDG Indonesia One. https://ptsmi.co.id/sdg-indonesia-one/.

Government of New Zealand, Department of Conservation. 2020. $1.1 Billion Investment to Create 11,000 Environment Jobs in Our Regions. https://www.doc.govt.nz/news/media-releases/2020-media-releases/investment-to-create-11000-environment-jobs-in-our-regions/.

Government of the Philippines, Department of Budget and Management. 2018. Green, Green, Green Pushes City Governments to Build Better Open Spaces. 27 June. https://dbm.gov.ph/index.php/secretary-s-corner/press-releases/list-of-press-releases/1092-green-green-green-pushes-city-governments-to-build-better-open-spaces.

Government of the United States, Department of Commerce, National Oceanic and Atmospheric Administration. 2020. Ocean Acidification. https://www.noaa.gov/education/resource-collections/ocean-coasts/ocean-acidification.

Grover, S., H. Rahemtulla, and C. Gin. "Managing Public–Private Partnerships for a Post Pandemic Recovery." ADB Blog. 29 May 2020. https://blogs.adb.org/blog/managing-public-private-partnerships-post-pandemic-recovery.

Hepburn, C. et al. 2020. Will COVID-19 fiscal recovery packages accelerate or retard progress on climate change? *Oxford Smith School of Enterprise and the Environment Working Paper* 20-02. 4 May. https://www.smithschool.ox.ac.uk/publications/wpapers/workingpaper20-02.pdf.

Howard, C. R. and N. F. Fletcher. 2012. Emerging Virus Diseases: Can We Ever Expect the Unexpected? *Emerg Microbes Infect.* 1 (12). pp. 1–9. 26 December. https://www.ncbi.nlm.nih.gov/pmc/articles/PMC3630908/.

Imperial College. 2020. Converting Emerging Markets to Green Finance: Amundi and the IFC. March. https://imperialcollegelondon.app.box.com/s/eg1002yc3un1g56nksug5vu4dnpeic1c.

International Capital Market Association. Green, Social, and Sustainability Bonds. https://www.icmagroup.org/green-social-and-sustainability-bonds/.

International Energy Agency. 2019. *Southeast Asia Energy Outlook 2019. Country Report.* October. https://www.iea.org/reports/southeast-asia-energy-outlook-2019.

International Monetary Fund. 2020. Confronting the Crisis: Priorities for the Global Economy. 9 April. https://www.imf.org/en/News/Articles/2020/04/07/sp040920-SMs2020-Curtain-Raiser.

International Renewable Energy Agency. 2016. *Renewal Energy Outlook for ASEAN.* https://www.irena.org/publications/2016/Oct/Renewable-Energy-Outlook-for-ASEAN.

Kelly, E. 2020. Germany Unveils €50B Stimulus for "Future-Focused" Technologies. *Science Business.* https://sciencebusiness.net/covid-19/news/germany-unveils-eu50b-stimulus-future-focused-technologies.

Koplitz, S. N. et al. 2017. Burden of Disease from Rising Coal-Fired Power Plant Emissions in Southeast Asia. *American Chemical Society.* 51 (3). pp. 1467–1476. https://pubs.acs.org/doi/full/10.1021/acs.est.6b03731.

Lamy, P. et al. 2020. Greener After: A Green Recovery Stimulus for a Post-COVID-19 Europe. *Jacques Delors Institute Policy Paper 200514.* https://institutdelors.eu/publications/greener-after/.

Loan Market Association (LMA). 2018. *Green Loan Principles.* United Kingdom. December. https://www.lma.eu.com/application/files/9115/4452/5458/741_LM_Green_Loan_Principles_Booklet_V8.pdf.

———. 2019. Sustainability Linked Loan Principles. United Kingdom. March. https://www.icmagroup.org/assets/documents/Regulatory/Green-Bonds/LMASustainabilityLinkedLoanPrinciples-270919.pdf.

Mace, M. 2019. Europe's "Man on the Moon Moment:" Green Deal to Create World's First Climate-Neutral Continent." *Edie.net.* 11 December. https://www.edie.net/news/11/Europe-s--man-on-the-moon-moment---Green-Deal-to-create-world-s-first-climate-neutral-continent/.

McKinsey & Company and Ocean Conservancy. 2017. *Stemming the Tide: Land-Based Strategies for a Plastic-Free Ocean.* https://oceanconservancy.org/wp-content/uploads/2017/04/full-report-stemming-the.pdf.

NBC News. 2007. Costa Rica gets largest debt-for-nature swap. 17 October. http://www.nbcnews.com/id/21345405/ns/world_news-world_environment/t/costa-rica-gets-largest-debt-for-nature-swap/#.X1XuTdZS9Z2.

Organisation for Economic Co-operation and Development. 2017. *Employment Implications of Green Growth: Linking Jobs, Growth, and Green Policies.* June. https://www.oecd.org/environment/Employment-Implications-of-Green-Growth-OECD-Report-G7-Environment-Ministers.pdf .

Pandjaitan, L. B. 2020. Here's How Indonesia Plans to Take on Its Plastic Pollution Challenge. World Economic Forum. 20 January. https://www.weforum.org/agenda/2020/01/here-s-how-indonesia-plans-to-tackle-its-plastic-pollution-challenge/.

Rankin, J. 2020. "Defining Moment" as EU Executive Pushes for €500bn in grants. *The Guardian*. https://www.theguardian.com/world/2020/may/27/defining-moment-coronavirus-as-eu-executive-pushes-for-500bn-in-grants.

Responsible Investor and Credit Suisse. 2020. Investors and the Blue Economy. Ocean risk or opportunity? Is the Blue Economy investible? https://www.esg-data.com/blue-economy.

Rey, A. 2010. REC Seeks RBI Approval to Sell Zero-Coupon Bonds to Bank. *Economic Times*. 18 November. https://economictimes.indiatimes.com/markets/bonds/rec-seeks-rbi-approval-to-sell-zero-coupon-bonds-to-banks/articleshow/6944443.cms?utm_source=contentofinterest&utm_medium=text&utm_campaign=cppst.

Robins, N., A. Pinzon, and M. Hugman. 2020. How Could Sustainable Finance Help Avoid an Emerging Market Sovereign Debt Crunch. The London School of Economics and Political Science. Grantham Research Institute on Climate Change and the Environment. 26 May. http://www.lse.ac.uk/granthaminstitute/news/how-could-sustainable-finance-help-avoid-an-emerging-market-sovereign-debt-crunch/.

Shahbandeh, M. 2018. Global Seafood Market Value 2016–2023. *Statista*. 27 March. https://www.statista.com/statistics/821023/global-seafood-market-value/.

Shalal, A. 2020. IMF Leader Says Pandemic Stimulus Must Focus on Battling Climate Crisis. *Reuters*. 29 April. https://in.reuters.com/article/us-health-coronavirus-imf-climate-idINKBN22B1OV.

Simon, F. 2020. Financiers Join EU "Green Recovery Alliance." Euractive.com. 5 May. https://www.euractiv.com/section/energy-environment/news/financiers-join-eu-green-recovery-alliance/.

———. 2020. EU Boosts "just transition fund," Pledging €40 Billion to Exit Fossil Fuels." *Euractive.com*. 28 May. https://www.euractiv.com/section/energy/news/eu-boosts-just-transition-fund-pledging-e40-billion-to-exit-fossil-fuels/.

Simpkins, K. 2020. Ocean Acidification Prediction Now Possible Years in Advance. *Science Daily*. https://www.sciencedaily.com/releases/2020/05/200501092916.htm.

Smith School of Enterprise and the Environment. 2020. Building Back Better: A Net-Zero Emissions Recovery. https://www.smithschool.ox.ac.uk/news/articles/200505-building-back-better-net-zero-emissions-recovery.html.

Sriring, O. 2020. Thailand Plans $33 Billion Public–Private Investment Projects. *Reuters*. 15 April. https://www.reuters.com/article/us-thailand-economy-investment/thailand-plans-33-billion-public-private-investment-projects-idUSKCN21X1PF.

Subacchi, P. 2020. A Covid-19 Debt Shock in Asia? *Australian Strategic Policy Institute The Strategist*. 2 June. https://www.aspistrategist.org.au/a-covid-19-debt-shock-in-asia/.

United Nations Environment Programme (UNEP). World Environment Day. Our Planet is Drowning in Plastic Pollution. https://www.unenvironment.org/interactive/beat-plastic-pollution/.

————. 2019. *Emissions Gap Report 2019*. https://wedocs.unep.org/bitstream/handle/20.500.11822/30797/EGR2019.pdf?sequence=1&isAllowed=y.

UNEP and DBS. 2017. *Green Finance Opportunities in ASEAN*. www.dbs.com/iwov-resources/images/sustainability/img/Green_Finance_Opportunities_in_ASEAN.pdf.

United Nations Framework Convention on Climate Change. 2017. Human Health and Adaptation: Understanding Climate Impacts on Health and Opportunities for Action. Synthesis Report by the Secretariat. Subsidiary Body for Scientific and Technological Advice 46th Session. Bonn. 8–18 May. https://unfccc.int/sites/default/files/resource/docs/2017/sbsta/eng/02.pdf.

————. 2019. Impacts of Climate Change on Sustainable Development. 19 July. https://unfccc.int/news/impacts-of-climate-change-on-sustainable-development-goals-highlighted-at-high-level-political-forum.

United Nations Office for Disaster Risk Reduction, Centre for Research on the Epidemiology of Disasters. 2018. *Economic Losses, Poverty and Disasters: 1998–2017*. https://www.unisdr.org/files/61119_credeconomiclosses.pdf.

United States Agency for International Development (USAID). Financing Forest Conservation: An Overview of the Tropical Forest and Coral Reef Conservation Act. https://www.usaid.gov/tropical-forest-conservation-act.

Van, P. 2020. Covid-19 Could Bankrupt 50% of Vietnamese Enterprises: VCCI. *VNExpress International*. 9 April. https://e.vnexpress.net/news/business/economy/covid-19-could-bankrupt-50-pct-of-vietnamese-enterprises-vcci-4081637.html.

Waite, R., T. Searchinger, and J. Ranganathan. "6 Pressing Questions About Beef and Climate Change." WRI Blog. 8 April 2019. https://www.wri.org/blog/2019/04/6-pressing-questions-about-beef-and-climate-change-answered.

Willis, T. J., R. B. Millar, and R. C. Babcock. 2003. Protection of Exploited Fishes in Temperate Regions: High Density and Biomass of Snapper *Pagrus auratus* (Sparidae) in Northern New Zealand Marine Reserves. *Journal of Applied Ecology*. 40. pp. 214–227. 8 April. https://pdfs.semanticscholar.org/9194/e92309612dba1a183153dff7bb40eba6a7e9.pdf.

World Economic Forum. 2020. *Radically Reducing Plastic Pollution in Indonesia: A Multistakeholder Action Plan National Plastic Action Partnership*. April. https://globalplasticaction.org/wp-content/uploads/NPAP-Indonesia-Multistakeholder-Action-Plan_April-2020.pdf.

World Economic Forum and AlphaBeta. 2020. *The Future of Nature and Business*. http://www3.weforum.org/docs/WEF_The_Future_Of_Nature_And_Business_2020.pdf.

World Economic Forum and SYSTEMIQ. 2020. *The Future of Nature and Business Policy Companion*. 14 July. https://www.weforum.org/reports/the-future-of-nature-and-business-policy-companion.

World Health Organization. 2018. One-third of Global Air Pollution Deaths in Asia Pacific. 2 May. https://www.who.int/westernpacific/news/detail/02-05-2018-one-third-of-global-air-pollution-deaths-in-asia-pacific.

www.ingramcontent.com/pod-product-compliance
Lightning Source LLC
Chambersburg PA
CBHW051657210326
41518CB00026B/2618